BUSINESS COMMUNICATION

TECHNIQUES AND METHODS

OM P JUNEJA
AARATI MUJUMDAR

Orient BlackSwan

Every attempt is being made to trace copyright holders for some graphic and textual materials used in this book, and the publishers and authors would be grateful for information on copyright holders so that due acknowledgement can be made in future editions of this book.

ORIENT BLACKSWAN PRIVATE LIMITED

Registered Office
3-6-752 Himayatnagar, Hyderabad 500 029 (A.P.) INDIA
E-mail: centraloffice@orientblackswan.com

Other Offices
Bangalore, Bhopal, Bhubaneshwar, Chandigarh, Chennai, Ernakulam, Guwahati, Hyderabad, Jaipur, Kolkata, Lucknow, Mumbai, New Delhi, Noida, Patna

First published 2010

Cover and book design

ISBN 978 81 250 4036 1

Typeset in Revival 565 10.5/13 *by*
OSDATA, Hyderabad 500 029

Printed in India at
Sri Kalanjali Graphics Hyderbad

Published by
Orient Blackswan Private Limited
3-6-752 Himayatnagar, Hyderabad 500 029 (A.P.) INDIA
E-mail: hyderabad@orientblackswan.com

Contents

Preface

It has become imperative for every professional to possess effective communication skills. It is essential to be technically sound; but expertise in one's specialisation alone does not ensure progress in one's career. It is extremely important that the ability to convey ideas effectively, in the simplest possible manner is developed.

Today, business is no longer localised in any one region or country; it is spread far and wide. Setting up business ventures in various provinces and countries amounts to dealing with different people speaking different languages, following various customs and cultures, diverse lifestyles, and dissimilar approaches and attitudes towards business. In addition, multiple time zones need to be taken cognizance of. Successful communication in these new markets require developing new skills such as cultural sensitivity, as well as a readiness to be flexible and tolerant and accepting of other people's points of view.

Therefore providing training in soft skills and developing sensitivity towards other cultures in students assumes importance. Unfortunately in India, this component seldom features in our academic curricula; as a result, the personality of the student is not adequately developed to cope with these new demands. Recognising the importance of these skills in today's competitive world, the UGC has now introduced Communication Skills as a part of its model curriculum for students across various disciplines. Even the CBSE has introduced courses of spoken English at schools. Hence, the main purpose of writing this book is, firstly to teach basic communication skills to learners, and secondly to nurture and polish the soft skills necessary for effective communication in learners.

This book incorporates nearly all the topics prescribed by the UGC. It is totally learner centric and inclusive of spoken and written components. Latest theories and approaches to communication including that of Thomas Freedman are incorporated in the book. A key text in understanding the social, economic and political implications of globalisation, Manuel Castell *Network Society*, has also been incorporated in the discussion in this book. These theoretical inputs will provide a firm foundation to students and the activities at the end of each unit will help them apply these theories to practical workplace situations.

The ability to read, listen, speak and write effectively are not innate. Hence, this book meticulously and systematically, teaches learners to cultivate, develop and hone these skills. As e-mails have become the preferred method of communication in business contexts, a chapter has been devoted to discussing this form of communication. The unit on listening skills emphasises the development of the art listening which is taken for granted and has therefore often been neglected. Presenting one's views on any topic requires careful planning and stratagem. The unit on presentations suggests various techniques that will help students get over the anxiety and nervousness associated with making presentations. The book also illustrates how a presentation can be enhanced if appropriate visuals are used. Group discussions develop in an individual, skills of interaction and negotiation, leadership qualities and inculcate a tolerance of others viewpoints. Techniques and suggestions are provided on how to behave and conduct oneself with team members and how to contribute successfully to a discussion. The unit on CVs, covering letters and professional documents would help learners to project themselves better when they enter the job market. To secure a job, knowledge of interview techniques is a must. It is hoped that the unit on this skill would help students face the interview panel with confidence and poise.

The book has special activities in each chapter to facilitate both teaching and learning. The teacher can make the whole class participate in the learning process and by undertaking these activities students can apply the theories learnt to actual business situations. This would help them develop an analytical approach; their problem-solving abilities and application skills would also be tested and sharpened.

The language used in this book is extremely learner and user friendly.

The work place is undergoing profound changes and hence individuals constantly need to upgrade themselves. Even if one has the knowledge of these skills there is always scope for improvement. This book is the outcome of our sincere endeavour to equip hard working, honest and competent learners with various skills so that they can find a place for themselves in this competitive job market and shaky economy.

Om Juneja
Aarati Mujumdar

List of Figures

List of Tables

Other titles from Orient BlackSwan

English Grammar in Steps: *D. Bolton and N. Goodey*

English Grammar in Steps: Practice Book: *D. Bolton and N. Goodey*

English Practice: *S. D. Joshi*

Enriching Oral and Written Communication in English: *Thorat and Lokhandwala*

Functional Grammar and Spoken and Written Communication in English: *Bikram K. Das*

Spoken English: A Foundation Course: Parts 1 and 2 (with audio CD): *K. Sadanand and S. Punita*

Strengthen your Writing: *V. R. Narayanswamy*

Synergy: Communication in English and Study Skills: *Board of Editors*

Textbook of Business Communication: *A. Kalkar, et al.*

Written Communication in English: *S. Freeman*

Chapter 1

Introduction to Business Communication

INTRODUCTION

In today's world, with almost universal trade and business practices, communication has acquired a place of prominence it has never assumed before. Globalisation, liberalisation, and democracy, that define today's world economic and political systems, depend heavily on communication. A good communicator is generally successful not only in professional dealings but also in personal relationships. Communication thus, is central to all the activities of society.

How one communicates ones thoughts, ideas and emotions to others is integral to striking a deal, negotiating a business, and putting it on paper before it is executed. It is important that what one wants to communicate, is conveyed in a lucid, simple, precise and matter-of-fact manner so that there is no misunderstanding and the goal is achieved. The pace at which ideas and thoughts are communicated matters in the process of decision making. In the highly competitive global market of today, communication skills are essential tools to establish one's credibility and identity. In short, being social animals, we are constantly communicating—at home with our family, at work with our co-workers and at leisure with our friends. We thus, share a social space with others through verbal and non-verbal communication at the local, national, and international levels.

Meaning of Communication

Accepting that communication is an important and an integral aspect of human life, what then does the term 'communication' actually mean? Human communication is the process by which thoughts and feelings of one person are conveyed to others with the help of verbal and non-verbal symbols. This process also involves giving and receiving information, persuading others and improving human relationships. In spite of many technologically advanced tools used in communication, language remains the most important.

Communication has been in existence since pre-historic times, as it is a basic need of human beings. The people of the Stone Age living in caves satisfied this need by carving figures on cave walls to communicate with other human beings. As human civilisation developed further, people who established communication networks succeeded in building empires. Papyrus, a kind of paper made out of the papyrus plant, played an important role in the formation and running of the ancient Egyptian, Greek and Roman empires because the kings sent orders written on these papers. This established a strong line of command between the rulers and their armies.

As the skills of writing developed, the use of signs and symbols to transmit messages also developed and with the passing of time, these were replaced with words that led to written script.

Initially, communication meant public speaking or oratory, in which rhetoric and speech were emphasised. With the inter-disciplinary approach gaining strength in the study of communication, psychologists and sociologists are of the opinion that not only verbal skills, but attitudes, persuasive skills and behavioural changes also create an impact on communication. Thus, the scope of 'communication' has broadened in its meaning to include transfer or sharing of knowledge, important ideas, and attitudes. In short, it means an exchange of meaningful information in an effective way.

DEFINING COMMUNICATION

Analysing some of the definitions of communication, we notice a gradual change in its meaning over the years. Keith Davis (1972) defined it as,

> . . . the transfer of information and understanding from one person to another, one business organisation to another. It is a way of reaching others with facts, ideas, thoughts and values. It is a bridge of meaning among people so that they can share what they feel and know. By using this bridge a person can cross safely the river of misunderstanding that sometimes separates people.

This definition makes some important observations which have been listed below.

a. Communication involves a minimum of two people, the sender and the receiver.
b. The sender transmits/conveys/sends the message to establish common and shared knowledge.
c. Knowledge can be shared only if the receiver understands the meaning of the message, which means that understanding the meaning of the message is as crucial as its transference.
d. While communicating, there are chances of misunderstandings that may occur due to misinterpretation of the message.

Communication thus builds a bridge of understanding between the sender and the receiver of the message. This definition does not talk about the role that 'attitude' plays in the process of sending and receiving messages.

The American Management Association defines communication as any behaviour which results in an exchange of meaning. As this is a very broad definition, some social scientists, are of the opinion that communication is mutual exchange of facts, thoughts, and perceptions, resulting in common understanding between the sender and the receiver. This definition, as you can see, is an improvement on Keith Davis's definition because here:

a. communication is considered a two-way process;
b. it is purposeful, and
c. it involves thoughts, feelings, and emotions.

This, however, does not cover all the components of the complexity of communicating in today's world.

Communication is purposive, asserts G. T. Vardaman in his book *Effective Communication of Ideas* (1970). For him, 'effective communication is a purposive symbolic interchange, resulting in workable understanding and agreement between sender and receiver.' This definition, lays emphasis on three important aspects of communication. They have been listed below.

a. Communication is goal oriented. For communication to be effective, communication needs to be goal oriented, which means that the message sent needs to have a pre-determined objective.
b. Communication should have a shared code. The message needs to be codified in such a way that a corpus of shared code is established between the sender and the receiver of the message. This corpus of shared code/language helps the receiver to understand the meaning of the message, which in turn could translate into feedback from the receiver in terms of an action or an appropriate response.
c. Communication should provide a feedback. The impact created by the message forms an integral and important component of effective communication. This is called feedback and is very useful in creating healthy business relations and consumer friendly practices.

Let us now look at a comprehensive definition given by Vardaman and Halterman in *Managerial Control through Communication* (1968).

> By communication we mean the flow of material, information, perception and understanding between various parts and members of an organisation...all the methods and means and media of communication (communication technology), all the channels, network and systems of communication (organisational structure) all the person-to-person interchange (interpersonal

communication)...it includes all aspects of communication: up, down, lateral, speaking, writing, listening, reading, methods, media, modes, channels, networks, flow, interpersonal, inter-organisational.

This definition highlights all the three important aspects of an effective communication: mode, channel and means of communication. When all these aspects are given due importance, the ensuing communication produces the desired results.

It can thus be surmised that the meaning of 'communication' has changed from mere oratory or rhetoric to making meaning of what is being said or conveyed. It has become a complex phenomenon in today's world in which English is used as *lingua franca* (a common language used by speakers of different languages) whereby it is shared among many groups of native speakers and is used as a common language by non-native speakers of different languages. It has also become the language of the international networks, financial markets, transnational corporations, the Internet, scientific and scholarly discourses, and a host of other transnational transactions. As the cultures of the two speakers in these communications differ because of their linguistic differences, using different socio-cultural and psychological approaches and methods, communication takes place in a complex social and business space.

In order to understand the complexity of communication in today's world, we may identify the following components of communication for further analysis. They are: a. sender, b. receiver, c. message, d. context, e. channel, f. culture and social/business space, and g. feedback or impact. There are several theories of communication, which analyse the role that these components play in making communication effective. We will briefly discuss some of them here.

THE SPEECH-ACT THEORY

The above components bear resemblance to the Speech-Act Theory, which links utterances (what the sender says) to the acts performed (the action that the receiver takes after decoding the sender's message). This also suggests that the meaning of the message can vary and change according to the situation, context, language and culture of the sender's utterance. Thus, communication does not take place in a vacuum or arbitrarily; it conforms to certain rule-based behaviours, norms and etiquette that are binding to both the sender and the receiver. Following the cooperative principle of H. P. Grice, any piece of conversation or a dialogue is an outcome of interrelated utterances that occur due to the cooperative behaviour of two or more persons. Each of them recognises what the outcome of this exchange is likely to be and tries to carry it forward to its expected closure. To attain this expected closure, Grice suggests four maxims of quantity, quality, relevance, and manner. Explaining them further, he asserts that the quantum of communication has to be just enough, neither too much nor too little, so that the receiver can draw out the core meaning of the sender's utterances. Similarly, on the sender's part, the utterances should not be irrelevant on matters he/she is trying to put across. The facts should be truthful with substantial amount of evidence to convince the receiver. Finally, the utterances made by the sender should be brief, orderly and precise without being obscure and ambiguous.

Thus, in an interaction or exchange, if either the sender or the receiver flouts even one of the maxims, it results in misunderstanding and misinterpretation of the message. In such a situation, both the sender and the receiver are faced with the dilemma of not knowing who is correct and what the other wants. In this situation the interaction may take another direction which neither of them would like. It may not result in the exchange of any concrete idea or message. It is important, therefore, to remember that each exchange is a result of the previous exchange of utterances. Thus, interactions taking place in accordance with Grice's cooperative principles help the sender and the receiver to achieve their goals.

Models of Communication

Communication has grown and developed over many years and these years have seen many models. The Greek philosopher

Aristotle in his treatise *Rhetoric* gave one of the earliest scientific models of communication to us. His simple model includes a sender, a receiver, and a message. He, however, emphasises the role of 'rhetoric', the persuasive power of the sender in bringing about a change in the thinking process of the receiver. In this model, the source or the sender is of primary importance thus making communication a one-way process. The ancient societies being autocratic and feudal, communication was generally one way and an honest dissenter, if allowed, could only use his/her oral rhetorical skills to plead or persuade. There was no scope to establish a channel for a two-way communication necessary in today's world. Scarcity of medium of communication also did not allow the sender to consider it necessary to ascertain whether the receiver had understood his/her message.

Harold Laswell extended the scope of Aristotle's model by including and laying emphasis on the channel of communication. Like Aristotle, his model too describes communication as a one-way transmission. A speaker sends a message and listeners receive the information that constitutes the message. The channel or medium of communication provides a point of contact between the speaker and the audience. The speaker thus creates some impact or effect upon the listener. The channel of communication, which Laswell includes in his model, is the medium of transmission as it provides a link between the source of information (the speaker/sender) and the destination (the listener/receiver). **Laswell's model** can be represented as shown below.

WHO says WHAT in what CHANNEL to WHOM in what CONTEXT with what EFFECT

FIGURE 1 Laswell's Model of Communication

As it is a linear model, it is not free from criticism. The principal criticism against this model is that it is limited to explaining how messages are sent to a destination. It does not tell us about the way the listeners may affect the speaker because it presumes a response. There is no place for feedback in this model. This model, therefore, does not deal with communication as a two-way process of give and take between a speaker and an audience of listeners. Hence, the linear model is concerned only with the transmission of information and how channels of communication were used to send and receive messages.

In the **Shannon and Weaver's model** shown below, a message begins at an information source, which is relayed through a transmitter, after it is sent via a signal towards the receiver. However, before it reaches the receiver, the message goes through 'noise' (sources of interference). Finally, the transmitter conveys the message to the receiver and thus ends at its destination. Even the Shannon–Weaver's model of communication is linear in nature and does not have feedback component as depicted in the figure given below.

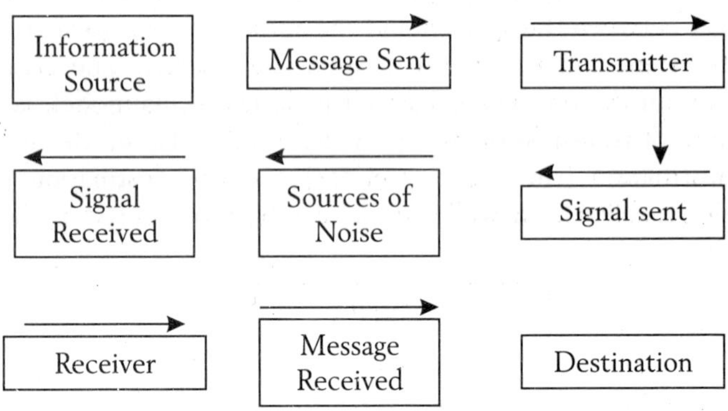

FIGURE 2 Shannon–Weaver's Model of Communication

Suppose you have an idea (information source) that you want to convey, you must first move the idea from your brain to your mouth (transmitter). Since you cannot actually share your grey matter, which is in your brain, you must select words for your transmitter to use. Once you speak the words, your voice (signal) is carried through the air towards the listener's ear (receiver). Along the way, your signal is joined by myriad other sounds and distractions (noises). The receiver takes in everything it receives and tries to maximise the message and minimise the noise. Finally, the receiver conveys the message to the listener's mind (destination).

This model highlights the role played by other sounds and distractions in the communication of messages. It clearly demonstrates why even the simplest communication can be misunderstood. Transmitting a signal across additional media only adds to the complexity of the communication and increases chance for distortion. This model helps us to understand why sometimes when we try to convey a message it is so difficult for people to understand what we already know. The model also underlines the role of language as a means of communication.

Modifications have been made to this model by adding the feedback component making way for the **interactive model**. This model describes communication as a two-way process as it incorporates feedback. While the interactive model is a refinement of the transmission/linear model because of the addition of feedback, it is, however, limited only to the transmission and reception of information. These models do not deal with how the messages are interpreted by receivers.

This issue of interpretation of messages has been addressed in a refined version of the interactive model, known as the **transactive model of communication**. It includes creation of the meaning of the message based on the frames of reference of the communicating participants. These communicating participants, in turn, produce a shared creation of meaning. In this process, the speaker and the listener simultaneously encode and decode messages received from one another on the basis of the frames of reference that each of them brings to the situation. This was a significant departure from the linear and the interactive models.

Let us now understand how the transactive model explains the process of creating and interpreting messages. First, each member of the audience brings his/her frame of reference to the speaking situation. That frame of reference is the sum of the experiences in the form of each person's knowledge, beliefs, and values, which are influenced by the culture to which they belong. Based on this corpus of personal knowledge, each member of the audience decodes the message. As members of the audience differ, their interpretations of messages are also likely to be different.

Secondly, based on the diversity of experiences the members of the audience bring to the situation, the speaker must construct the message in such a way that he has a meaningful dialogue with the audience members. The speaker must, therefore, prepare the message based on the following:

a. areas of shared frame of references with the greatest number of people in the audience,
b. shared beliefs and values that could be agreed upon by the maximum number of people and
c. the differences among the members of the audience, because each person brings to the speaking situation a distinctive set of personal experiences. Kenneth Burke uses the term 'identification' to describe the rhetorical strategy of emphasising all those areas of common ground that a speaker uses.

To sum up, we have so far discussed three types of models of human communication. They are:

a. the linear model that focuses on the transmission of information;
b. the interactive model that features two-way communication through the feedback loop; and
c. the transactive model that emphasises how communicators create meaning based on their shared frame of reference.

We will now deal with the actual process of communication and how it happens in everyday life.

THE COMMUNICATION PROCESS

Communication is no doubt central to the knowledge economy and is a major consideration for anyone entering the work place.

However, its meaning is not limited to only transmission and transference of information and meaning from an individual or a group to another individual or a group. The most crucial element/ factor embedded in this definition is 'meaning'—how it is communicated and how much of it has been deciphered. Effective communication, therefore, means 'successful transference and transmission of meaning'. In fact, the process of communication is considered successful only when the receiver understands the message as the sender had intended it. Both, the sender and the receiver must agree not only on the information transmitted and transferred but also on the underlying meaning that it conveys. Therefore, the linear models of Laswell and Shannon and Weaver do not serve our purpose, as they do not include the response generated by the receiver. Feedback or response generated by the receiver needs to be transmitted and transferred back to the sender for the latter to understand whether the meaning has been conveyed or not. This necessarily means that communication is a two-way process.

Communication, thus, is the process of passing information and understanding from one person to another. This communication process involves six basic elements: sender (encoder), message, channel, receiver (decoder), noise, and feedback. We can improve communication skills by becoming aware of these elements and how they contribute to successful communication. Communication can break down when any of these elements is missing at any level.

As the following figure suggests the **sender** initiates the communication process. The sender may be an individual or a group, or a large mass of people. It could also include mass media, a business house, government, educational, religious, or cultural organisations, etc. When the sender has decided on an idea/ thought to be conveyed keeping in mind its purpose and objective for its transmission, he/she **encodes** a message, and selects a channel for transmitting the message to a receiver. To encode is to put an idea/thought into words, images, or symbols, which would be acceptable to the receiver. It is only after encoding that an idea takes the form of a message. Encoding thus is a process of packaging an idea into a message to be conveyed.

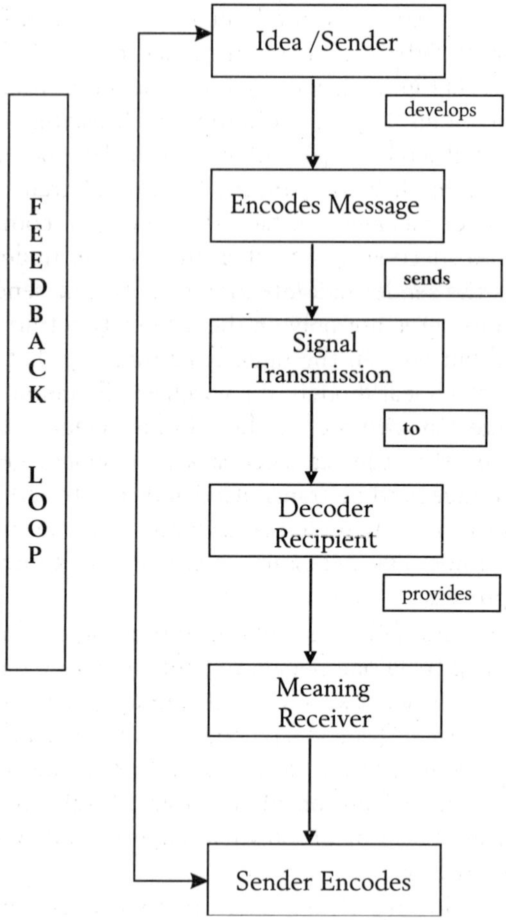

FIGURE 3 The Process of Communication

The **message,** therefore, is the information that the sender wants to transmit. The **medium/channel** is the means of communication, such as spoken, written, electrical, digital, etc. Depending on the purpose of the message, the sender selects the best medium that suits it. This message can be transmitted either through verbal communication on a one-to-one, face-to-face basis or through a telephone or if it requires writing then through a letter, a telegram, a memo, a diagram, in figures, charts, or through an e-mail. People can even transmit messages through non-verbal communication such as signs, actions, facial expressions, eye movements, gestures, etc. We shall discuss these components in detail in another unit.

Generally, both non-verbal and verbal channels of communication are used to transact business. For example, when two persons or parties reach a basic agreement on an issue at a meeting through discussion or a conversation on the telephone, they put a seal of confirmation on the deal with a written communication through an e-mail or a letter. This type of communication is generally used for the purpose of inquiring, ordering goods or even to minimise time on taking important decisions.

The **receiver** is a person or a group of people for whom the communication is intended. The receiver has to be ready for the message and attentive to it so that the meaning can be decoded and interpreted by analysing the sender's role, knowledge, experience, and authority. He/she needs to translate the symbols and ideas into a form that can be understood. Accurate and effective communication can occur only when both, the sender and the receiver, attach the same or similar meanings to the symbols in the encoded and the decoded message.

Communication remains incomplete until the sender receives a response from the receiver, which is called **feedback**. It is the response of the receiver to the sender's message. The receiver decodes or makes meaning of the message and transfers information back to the sender. In the feedback loop, the initial roles get reversed. The receiver becomes the sender and the sender becomes the receiver. Such exchanges take place continually making communication a dynamic two-way process. Feedback, thus, ensures that mutual understanding has taken place in communication. It also provides means to evaluate the effectiveness of the message. Positive feedback suggests the effectiveness of the message while negative feedback informs the sender that his/her message has not resulted in the desired outcome. In a face-to-face communication feedback is immediate and it can be indicated through verbal or non-verbal means.

It is wrong to suppose that such exchanges take place smoothly without difficulties or problems, as there are numerous barriers in the way of effective communication. The most important barrier to communication is called **noise**, which may be defined as a distracting force that interferes in deciphering meaning. Though not present in the original message, it creeps in from the outside and distracts the concentration of both the sender and the receiver. 'Noise' can enter the process of communication due to some situational factors or the inability of the sender to encode the message in clear and understandable language. It may also happen because of the inability of the receiver to decode or interpret the sent message properly. Noise may also result from cultural differences between the sender and the receiver, and due to certain sounds made by the sender that are not known to the receiver. Some times, distortions may occur due to some physical problems such as a hearing impairment or a defective throat or mouth that results in the speaker not being able to utter certain sounds or pronounce some words and speak in certain intonation patterns. In short, noise may be caused due to the sender, the transmission or the receiver. Let us identify the distracting features and the various barriers/noises that come in the way of effective communication.

Barriers to Communication

Communication plays a major role in employer-employee relationships. Although effective communication does not guarantee the success of any business or enterprise, its absence, however, causes many problems. If not solved immediately or in time, this problem may soon become a crisis or may linger on for years. More specifically, the role of communication in any organisation or an enterprise influences the effectiveness of hiring, training, and motivating employees, providing daily instructions, evaluating performances and handling disciplinary problems. Effective communication skills, therefore, are essential for the health of the entire working community. Its absence affects the willingness of the employees to provide useful suggestions and inputs for the advancement of the business. In fact, effective communication between supervisors and employees is required for the latter to make the all-important transition from 'workers' to 'working managers'.

Thus, caution should be exercised in this regard. Sometimes the sender or the receiver adds barriers of communication consciously or unconsciously. If the speaker or the listener has any problems in adjusting to one another's frequency, barriers are erected. This hampers growth of communication and relegates it to the status of a conversation resulting in no feedback, no meaning making or understanding of the message.

Some of the important barriers that hamper communication are discussed below.

1. **Muddled Messages:** Effective communication starts with a clear message. Muddled messages are a barrier to communication because they leave the receiver unclear about the intent of the sender. Muddled messages have many causes. Generally, such messages are sent when the sender is confused. The message in such cases may be little more than a vague idea. Feedback from the receiver helps the sender to be sure that the message is clear and not muddled. Clarifying muddled messages is the responsibility of the sender.

2. **Stereotyping:** A stereotype is a conventional conception or image that typifies a person, a group, an event, or a thing on oversimplified conceptions, beliefs, or opinions. Stereotyping can substitute for thinking, analysis, and open mindedness to a new situation. It is therefore a barrier to communication when it causes people to act as if they already know the message that is coming from the sender. It is worse than that when people think that no message is necessary because 'everybody already knows'. Both the sender and the listener should continuously look for and account for thinking, conclusions, and actions based on stereotypes.

3. **Wrong channel:** If the sender uses the wrong channel to communicate then wrong signals are sent to the receiver/listener. For example, to greet someone 'Good morning', an oral channel

is very appropriate. However, if you write 'GOOD MORNING!' on a chalkboard or on a piece of paper and circulate it amongst your co-workers, it defeats the very purpose and effectiveness of the greeting. On the contrary, a detailed request to a contractor for handling any equipment on a site should be made in writing, not in oral form. Having a long conversation with the contractor without taking notes surely will result in confusion and misunderstanding. These simple examples illustrate how using the wrong channel can be a barrier to communication.

Variation of channels helps the receiver understand the nature and importance of a message. A written disciplinary warning emphasises the seriousness of the problem. In the choice of a channel, the sender needs to be sensitive to such things as the complexity of the message ('good morning' versus a construction contract); the consequences of a misunderstanding about the knowledge, skills and abilities of the receiver (a new employee versus a partner in the business); and immediacy of action to be taken from the message (instructions for the morning's work versus a plan of work for the year 2011).

4. **Language:** Words are not concrete reality. They are mental representations, as the receiver understands them combined with the shared perceptions of the sender. While language constitutes only the representation of the sound symbols, the rest is perception. Thus, the sender should not use an 'alien' or a 'foreign' language to transfer his/her message. He/she should use a language that is clearly understood by the receiver. Here the word 'foreign' or 'alien' does not mean a language of another country. It means any verbal or non-verbal language, which the receiver does not understand. If there is no shared language between the two then the message is likely to be misunderstood by the receiver/listener.

5. **Semantic problems:** These problems are related to the study of meaning or the changes of meaning, which occur when people use either the same word in different ways or different words in the same way. They also occur when people use jargon, a specialised technical terminology characteristic of a particular subject that

they expect others to understand or when they use language that is not within the vocabulary of the receiver. While sending messages, semantic problems can be avoided if the sender keeps in mind the language of the receiver.

6. **Lack of feedback:** Feedback reflects the message/idea that the sender has sent as the receiver perceives it. Without feedback, communication is a one-way process. The sender can get a feedback in many ways. Asking a person to repeat what has been said, is a very direct way of receiving the feedback. It is not always possible to receive feedback in this manner. It could also be as subtle as a stare, a nod of confirmation or a puzzled look from the listener, which conveys a failure in comprehension when complicated instructions have been given. Both the sender and the receiver can play an active role in using feedback to make communication a two-way process. Feedback should be helpful rather than hurtful. Prompt feedback is more effective than feedback saved up until the 'right' moment because it is likely that the right moment may never arise or when it arrives, it may be too late as the message is already misunderstood or misinterpreted. Feedback should be specific rather than general and should be considered a problem in perception not in discovering facts.

7. **Poor listening skills:** Listening is a difficult activity. An average speaker speaks about one hundred and twenty words per minute while a listener's mind can process about four hundred words per minute. This means that the mind of the listener is free for seventy-five percent of the time that he/she is being spoken to. In this free time the listener often gets sidetracked or distracted. The solution to this problem is to be an active listener rather than a passive one. Nevertheless, one cannot be an active listener unless one is prepared to listen. Thoughts about matters other than what's being spoken about should be discarded and the focus should be on searching for meaning in what the speaker is saying. The receiver should follow the following principles:

a. He/she must avoid interrupting the sender and should prepare a mental outline or summary of the important thoughts formed,

b. the receiver should also withhold evaluation, and judgment until the other person has finished sending the message.

A listener frowning, shaking his/her head, looking bored, etc. provides instant feedback, and can easily convince the sender that there is no reason to elaborate or try to communicate his or her idea again, notwithstanding the merit of the idea. The receiver has to be an animated listener and focus on what the other person is saying. Once the message has been sent by the sender and listened to by the receiver, a feedback should be provided.

8. **Interruptions:** An organisation or an office is a lively place. Even though a few days are routine, generally there is hectic activity among the employees to attain their targets and goals. In such an environment, casual conversations about last night's cricket match or a movie, etc. are likely to create interruptions. Interruptions could also be due to lack of time, lack of privacy, drop-in visitors, emergencies, or even the curiosity of someone wanting to know what two other people are saying. Regardless of the cause, interruptions are a barrier to communication that may perhaps result in giving incomplete instructions or in an incomplete discussion or a meeting. For effective communication, it is important that such interruptions be avoided.

9. **Physical distractions:** All the physical things that get in the way of communication are termed physical distractions. Examples of such things include the ringing of a telephone, insufficiently insulated rooms, poor lighting, noise of traffic, noise from a construction site in the vicinity, the whirring of air conditioners, the noise of a plane flying above the building, and an uncomfortable meeting place. These physical distractions are extremely common. If the phone rings, the tendency is to answer it even if the caller is interrupting a very important conversation. For a person sitting behind a desk, talking across the desk is talking from behind a physical barrier. Uncomfortable meeting places may include a place that has uncomfortable chairs, that is too hot or too cold. Noise too is a physical distraction simply because it is hard to concentrate on a conversation if hearing is difficult.

10. **Cultural differences:** These effect communication between people from different departments within the organisation, or between people who are from different cultural, social, and religious environments. Let us consider the difference between people in the Research and Development (R and D) department and the production department of an organisation. While the R and D people who are involved in research-based work have a vision for future expansion and quality of the products that the organisation is manufacturing, the people in the production department are more concerned with keeping its assembly line to meet their daily targets. Their work orientation thus creates cultural differences, which may lead to confusion and misunderstanding that may damage a negotiated settlement.

OVERCOMING THE BARRIERS

Summarising the process again, we can say that the communication process starts with a sender who has a message for a receiver. Thus, two or more people are always involved in communication. The sender's message travels to the receiver through one or more channels chosen by the sender. The channels may be verbal or non-verbal. They may involve only one of the senses (just hearing, for example), or involve all the five: hearing, sight, touch, smell, and taste. Non-verbal communication, popularly referred to as 'body language', relies primarily on seeing rather than hearing. The sending of a message by an appropriate channel to a receiver appears to have completed the communication least the sender's responsibility. After sending the message, the sender becomes a receiver and the receiver becomes a sender through the process of feedback. Feedback is the receiver's response to the attempt by the sender to send the message and the key to understanding whether the message has been received in the intended form or not. The channel for feedback may be quite different from the original channel chosen by the sender. A puzzled look also constitutes feedback, which the sender considers a perfectly clear oral instruction. Effect on the receiver completes the communication process. Hence, 'effective communication' means that the original sender has the desired effect on the receiver. Thus, communication at its best minimises misunderstanding between the sender and the receiver. Ineffective communication therefore means either there is no effect on the receiver or the effect is unexpected, undesired and/or unknown to the sender. This simplified explanation of a complex process can be a powerful tool for thinking about one's communication skills, diagnosing communication problems and developing plans for one's improvement.

One has to accept the fact that it is not easy to communicate effectively. Roadblocks are bound to occur at every stage. Despite this, one needs to move forward by reducing the effects of the barriers. The first step towards finding solutions is to remove specific barriers that hamper communication.

Look at the tips given below to overcome barriers in communication.

1. Have a positive attitude about communication. Defending your attitude interferes with communication.
2. Continuously work at improving communication skills. The communication model and discussion of barriers provide the necessary knowledge that can be used to develop an increased awareness of the potential to improve communication skills.
3. One must be conscious of the importance of effective communication as a skill that is evaluated along with other skills in the job market. Help other people improve their communication skills by helping them understand their communication problems.
4. Make communication goal oriented. Relational goals come first and pave the way for other goals. When the sender and the receiver have a good relationship, they are more likely to accomplish their communication goals than otherwise.
5. Communication should be approached as a creative process rather than as a regular chore. Experiment with communication alternatives. What works with one person may not work well with another. Use different channels and listening, and feedback techniques.

6. Accept the reality of miscommunication. Even the best communicators sometimes fail in sending a clean message. One must accept the possibility of miscommunication and work to minimising its negative impacts.

Summary

Communication is at the heart of many interpersonal problems. It is a fact faced by employers universally. Understanding the communication process and then working towards improvement, provide managers with the ability to become effective communicators. Knowing the common barriers is the first step towards minimising their impact. Students, who are tomorrow's managers, need to first question themselves on how effective they are as communicators. Further, they can reflect and take stock of their negatives, make use of the ideas presented in this chapter and shape themselves to be effective communicators in a globalised and a liberalised world economy.

Activities

1. Here is a simple activity to assess one's own communication skills. Circle the number from 1 to 5 (indicating low to high ability) that best represents your skills in a particular area.

Writing Skills

- Basic spelling, grammar, and punctuation skills [1 2 3 4 5]
- Familiarity with memo, letter, and report formats for business documents [1 2 3 4 5]
- Ability to analyse a writing problem and quickly outline a plan for solving the problem [1 2 3 4 5]
- Ability to organise data coherently and logically [1 2 3 4 5]
- Ability to evaluate a document to determine its probable success [1 2 3 4 5]

READING SKILLS

- Familiarity with general and specialised vocabulary in the field [1 2 3 4 5]
- Ability to concentrate despite distractions [1 2 3 4 5]
- Willingness to look up definitions whenever necessary [1 2 3 4 5]
- Ability to move from recreational to serious reading [1 2 3 4 5]
- Ability to read and comprehend academic material [1 2 3 4 5]

SPEAKING SKILLS

- Ease in speaking with friends [1 2 3 4 5]
- Ease at speaking in front of group of people [1 2 3 4 5]
- Ability to adapt presentation to the audience [1 2 3 4 5]
- Confidence in pronouncing and using words correctly [1 2 3 4 5]

LISTENING SKILLS

- Listening skills during conversations [1 2 3 4 5]
- Ability to concentrate on a speaker's words despite distractions [1 2 3 4 5]
- Ability to summarise the speaker's ideas and anticipate what is coming during pauses [1 2 3 4 5]

2. Imagine that you are Vice-President (Marketing) in a consumer goods organisation and you wish to announce a new policy aimed at improving customer service. Examine the entire communication process from the sender to the feedback and answer the following questions.
   a. What assumptions would you make of the customers?
   b. How would you encode the message?
   c. What channels would you use to communicate the message.
   d. How would you encourage feedback?

e. What barriers can you expect when you are disseminating the new customer service policy?

f. How do you plan to overcome those barriers?

3. No communication is successful unless the receiver understands the message as the sender intends its. Analyse the following examples of communication failures.

   a. The owner of Pooja Copying Centre issued the following announcement:

      'Effective immediately the charge of copying services will be raised by 50p to rupee each.'

   b. The pilot of a military airplane about to land decided that the runway was too short. He shouted to his engineer, 'Take off power'. The engineer turned off the engine and the plane crashed.

4. The following statements appeared in letters of application for an advertised job opening. Identify the errors in it and rewrite the statements again.

   a. Enclosed is my resume in response to Sunday's Times of India.

   b. Enclosed is my resume in response to my search for an editorial/creative position.

   c. My experience in the production of newsletters, magazines, directories and on-line data bases puts me head and shoulders above the crowd of applicants you have no doubtedly been inundated with.

The activities have been adapted from *Business Communication Process & Product* by Mary Allen Guffy.

REFERENCES

Davis, Keith. 1972. Human Relations at Work: *The Dynamics of Organizational Behavior*. New York: McGraw Hill.

Vardaman, George T. 1970. *Effective Communication of Ideas*. New York: Van Nostrand Reinhold Company.

Vardaman George T. and Carroll C. Halterman. 1968. *Managerial Control through Communication: Systems for Organizational Diagnosis and Design*. New York: Wiley.

Chapter 2

Communication in Organisations

INTRODUCTION

In the previous unit, we discussed the term 'communication' in a wide context. In this unit, communication will be analysed in the context of businesses, trade and commerce, industry and other institutions, where sharing of information takes place across national and international locations.

Creating and sharing knowledge, which is critical to fostering innovations, are the key challenges in this age of information. Manuel Castells (1996) talks about the age of information, 'informational economy', which depends on agents' capacity to efficiently generate, process, and apply knowledge-based information. This new economy, according to Castells, has emerged worldwide during the last two decades. The rise of this global, informational economy is mainly because of the knowledge base of the economy, its global reach, and the informational technology revolution.

The informational economy is global. This global economy is different from the industrial economy. While the industrial economy works within the given dimensions of time and space, the informational economy has the capacity to work as a unit in 'real time' on a planetary scale. It may be noted that 'real time' is the time it takes for a process under computer control to occur. Though the capitalist mode of production has been in existence for almost two centuries, it is only in the late twentieth century that the world economy was able to become truly global because of new infrastructure provided by information and communication technologies working in 'real time'. This globality concerns the core processes and elements of the economic system, which depend upon highly efficient and apt communication.

Industrial economy is orientated towards economic growth and maximisation of output, while the focus of the informational economy is on technological development and the accumulation of knowledge and higher levels of complexity in information processing. The growth of this new economic system, which is characterised by the pursuit of knowledge and information, has created informational society. Castells calls this society the 'network society' which is governed by a 'networking logic' of its own. It is a new social structure highly dependent on communication.

Improved systems of telecommunication, advanced forms of transportation and saturated local markets are some of the factors that have encouraged companies to move beyond familiar territories to emerging markets around the world. Pepsi fighting with Coco Cola for new customer base in Asia and Burger King challenging McDonald for fast food supremacy in Europe are common examples of companies vying for a bigger share in new markets.

Doing business across countries means dealing with people who are very different from one another in terms of religion, customs, habits, cultures, and living styles. More importantly, they have different approaches and styles of running a business. Different time zones, vast distances between offices, different spoken languages, etc. are some of the barriers in communication in this context.

In these emerging markets around the globe, successful communication between the negotiating parties is a must. This demands adequate verbal and non-verbal language skills, sensitivity towards culture, flexibility, patience, understanding, and tolerance. Even within an organisation, it is necessary that all the employees must be good communicators so that they can be moved from one location to another, within the country or internationally, if the need arises. With flattened management hierarchies and expanded team-based managements, every employee must be a skilled communicator as his/her work scope has become much larger than he/she was initially employed for. For example, a computer programmer has to do more than just code and debug. He has to listen, interpret, and explain to others. All members in an organisation have to analyse problems and negotiate solutions. Hence, it is important that there is a regular exchange of information within the organisation as well as with others outside the organisation.

COMMUNICATION IN ORGANISATIONS

The word 'communication' is derived from the Latin word 'communico' which means 'to share'. The art and craft of communication therefore is about creating a shared meaning. Communication, in fact, plays a role in creating reality. It is not a mere reflection of reality. As explained in the previous chapter, speaking, writing, or producing a text alone does not constitute communication. Communication is not simply a mechanical flow of knowledge or information; it involves values, power, status, and most importantly negotiation of meaning.

Communication, as discussed in the previous chapter, is undertaken either to reduce uncertainty, alter power relationships, solve problems, confirm beliefs, control the situation, or to provide feedback. As an organisation receives information externally or internally there are formal and informal channels of communication in an organisation. We shall discuss various channels of communication in the next unit. However, let us discuss, in brief, the meaning of external and internal communication.

External Communication

All types of communications sent out of an organisation are external communications. Such communication occurs between the organisations and customers, bankers, suppliers, insurance companies, government departments, mass media, and the general public. They may be in the form of letters, telephone calls, telegrams reports, advertisements, press handouts discussions, meetings and visits. Sending messages via e-mails, SMS and faxes to the concerned parties also constitute external communication. External functions include answering enquiries about products or services, persuading customers to buy products or services, clarifying supplier specifications, issuing credit, collecting bills, responding to government agencies, regulatory, legal or trade agencies and promoting a positive image of the organisation.

Similarly, every organisation receives inward communications from individuals/groups outside of the company in the form of letters, telephone calls, telegrams, reports, advertisements, press handouts, discussions, meetings, visits, e-mails, SMS messages, and faxes. Even brochures, journals, magazines, and circulars from government departments and other regulatory and legal bodies constitute inward communication. They have to be registered, attended to, studied, acted upon, replied and stored for ready reference.

Internal Communication

Varied and complex types of communications occur within an organisation between managers, supervisors, and workers. This type of communication is called internal communication, which aims at creating a conducive climate in the work place for higher productivity and excellence. Some of the functions of internal communication are to issue and clarify procedures and policies, inform management of progress, persuade employees or the management to make changes or improvements, coordinate activities and evaluate and reward employees. In all the internal and external tasks, employees and managers use all types of communication skills: reading, listening, speaking, thinking, and writing. There are a large number of diverse business communication functions and they can be summarised in the following three categories.

a. to inform
b. to persuade
c. to promote goodwill

The functions of business communication are graphically represented in the following box.

TABLE 1 Functions of Business Communication

To inform	
To persuade	
To practice goodwill	
Internal Communication with:	External Communication with:
Superiors	Customers
Coworkers	Suppliers
Subordinates	Government agencies The public

Source: Business Communication Process and Product by Mary Ellen Guffey

Interpersonal Communication

Interpersonal communication or dyadic communication refers to communication or interaction between two individuals. In this type of communication, emphasis is on transferring information and gearing towards construction of meaning. As a result, mutual trust, understanding and consideration are some of the positives that grow from such an interaction.

Interpersonal communication is also considered one of the basic factors effecting behavioural changes. Fred Luthans (1992) states that 'On one hand communication, incorporates the psychological processes of perception, learning and motivation and while it incorporates language on the other'. It encompasses listening, conversing, summarising, and paraphrasing. Non-verbal communication is also closely associated with this approach.

Any message can be analysed from two aspects—content and relationships. The content of a message can be objectively analysed by observing whether the message contains the information that is to be conveyed. This in turn would determine the effectivity of the communication. If the communication is missing the information that the receiver wants then we say that the information transmitted is devoid of content.

Relationships in messages often represent feelings in which non-verbal cues are emphasised more than verbal ones. In the process of communication, each one of us puts forward our own perspectives. The degree of closeness in a relationship is described by how accessible the people in the relationship are to each other. Communication becomes easier when we get to know and understand the people we are communicating with even when there are unshared perceptions, values, etc. An individual varies in accessibility with different people and when dealing with different issues. Many a times at the very first meeting with someone we think, 'I don't like this person; I can't get through to him/her'. First impressions always tend to last and we try to reject the cues that threaten our confidence in judging people. It is important to note that the quality of a relationship is directly related to the quantity and quality of information sharing.

The Johari Window

Ingham and Luft presented 'The Johari Window' to illustrate the vital role of relationship, in terms of awareness in sharing information, in the development and maintenance of interpersonal relationships. It lends itself as a self-teaching device in learning about human relationships and illustrates the manner in which we can increase objectivity in the way we perceive others and ourselves. It is useful in reducing bias in interpersonal relationships.

This model is also commonly referred to as the 'disclosure/feedback model of self awareness', and by some people as an 'information processing tool'. The Johari Window represents information—feelings, experience, views, attitudes, skills, intentions, motivations, etc.—within or about a person, in relation to their group, from four perspectives, which are described below. The model can also be used to represent the same information for a group in relation to other groups. Its terminology refers to 'self' and 'others': 'self' means oneself, or the person subject to the

Johari Window analysis, and 'others' means other people in the person's group or team.

1 open/free area	2 blind area
3 hidden area	4 unknown area

FIGURE 4 Johari Window 1

As shown in the above figure, the Johari window comprises four quadrants of equal size, each representing four aspects of an individual and the total personality of a person in relation to others.

Quadrant I—The area of free activity or public area (Arena / Open Area)

Johari region 1 is also known as the 'area of free activity'. This is the information about the person's behaviour, attitude, feelings, emotion, knowledge, experience, skills, views, etc., that is known to the person ('the self') and known to the group ('others'). When we interact with other people, we make apparent some attitudes and elements of our behavior and personality that WE know about ourselves. This type of interaction is marked by openness and compatibility. There is very little possibility of defensive behavior and feelings.

The aim of any group should always be to develop the 'open area' for every person in the group, because this ensures that each person in the group and the group as a whole is effective and productive. The open free area, or 'the arena', is the space where good communication and cooperation occurs, free from distractions, mistrust, confusion, conflict and misunderstanding.

Quadrant II—The blind area (Blind Spot)

Blind area refers to certain attitudes, motivations and feelings which are known to others, but unknown to self. Others can see and observe some facets of our personality of which we are unaware. For example, a person may be speaking too fast. This may cause some irritability in others but it is unintentional on the part of the speaker.

Quadrant III—The avoided or hidden areas (Façade/ Hidden Area)

Johari region 3 is what is known to ourselves but kept hidden from, and therefore unknown, to others. This hidden or avoided self represents information, feelings, etc., that a person knows about himself or herself, but does not revealed to others. The hidden area could include sensitivities, fears, hidden agendas, manipulative intentions, secrets, etc. It's natural for very personal and private information and feelings to remain hidden. Certain information, feelings and experiences have no bearing on work, and so can and should remain hidden. However, typically, a lot of hidden information is often official, and is work or performance-related. In such cases the information and so is better positioned in the open area.

Quadrant IV—Areas of unknown activity (Unknown Area/ Undiscovered Area)

The undiscovered self refers to those aspects of an individual that he/she does not understand or know about and are not apparent to others. It is likely that the concerned individual or others are aware of certain behaviours or motives. Yet, we can assume their existence because eventually some of these behaviours and motives do affect our behaviour and influence relationships. This form of behaviour is considered highly explosive. Examples of unknown factors are as follows; the first example is particularly relevant and common, especially in typical organisations and teams.

- an ability that is underestimated or untried through lack of opportunity, encouragement, confidence or training
- a natural ability or aptitude that a person doesn't realise they possess
- a fear or aversion that a person does not know they have
- an unknown illness
- repressed or subconscious feelings
- conditioned behaviour or attitudes from childhood

The proponents of this model explain that there are several principles governing changes within this Johari Window. These principles are listed below.

1. A change in any one quadrant will affect all other quadrants.
2. It takes energy to hide, deny, or to be blind to behaviour which is involved in interaction.
3. Threat tends to decrease awareness; mutual trust tends to increase awareness.
4. Forced awareness (exposure) is undesirable and usually ineffective.
5. Interpersonal learning means that a change has taken place so that quadrant I is larger, and one or more of the other quadrants has grown smaller.
6. Working with others is facilitated by many areas of free activity. This means more resources and skills can be applied to the task at hand.
7. The smaller the first quadrant, the poorer the communication.
8. There is universal curiosity about the unknown area but this is held in check by customs, social training, and by diverse fears.
9. Sensitivity means appreciating the covert aspects of behavior in quadrants II, III and IV and respecting the desire of others to keep them so.
10. Learning about group processes, as they are experienced, helps to increase awareness (larger quadrant I) for the group as a whole as well as for individual members.

11. The value system of a group and its members may be noted in the way the unknown aspects in the life of the group are confronted.

Apart from these principles, two major processes governing interpersonal relationships are 'disclosure' and 'feedback'. They cause redistribution of awareness and changes in the size and form of the four quadrants. They help the 'open-self quadrant' or the arena to become larger. This makes the relationship more rewarding and productive, revealing the dynamic and the sensitive nature of the model.

Disclosure and Feedback

The process of feedback and disclosure helps reduce the hidden-self quadrant and increase the 'open self' quadrant. Candid disclosure forms a strategy for sharing awareness with others. The size of the open area can be expanded horizontally into the blind space, by seeking and actively listening to feedback from other group members. This process is known as 'feedback solicitation'. Also, other members with whom the person interacts can help her/him to expand her/his open area by offering feedback, sensitively. The size of the open area can also be expanded vertically downwards into the hidden or avoided space by the person's disclosure of information, feelings, etc. about himself/herself to some other colleagues and peers with whom he/she interacts.

By seeking or soliciting feedback from others, the aim should be to reduce this area and increase the open area (see the diagram on page 36), that is, to increase self-awareness. This blind area is not an effective or a productive space for individuals or groups. The blind area could also include information that others are deliberately withholding from a person or a person is deluded about. We all know how difficult it can be to work well when kept in the dark. Therefore, it is very important that awareness of what is happening around oneself be increased.

Individuals can be helped to reduce their blind area—in turn increase the open area—by giving sensitive feedback and encouraging disclosure. Managers should promote a climate of non-judgemental feedback, and group response to individual disclosure, which reduces fear and therefore encourages both processes to happen. The extent to which an individual seeks feedback, and the issues on which feedback is sought, must always be at the individual's own discretion. Some people are more resilient than others are. Care needs to be taken to avoid causing emotional upset. The process of soliciting serious and deep feedback relates to the process of 'self-actualisation'.

It takes longer for quadrant II to reduce in size, because usually there are 'good' reasons of a psychological nature to blind ourselves to the things we feel or do. Relevant hidden information and feelings, etc., should be moved into the open area through the process of 'disclosure'. The aim should be to disclose and expose relevant information and feelings—which in the Johari Window terminology is called 'self-disclosure' and 'exposure process'–thereby increasing the open area. By telling others how we feel and other information about ourselves we reduce the hidden area, and increase the open area, which enables better understanding, cooperation, trust, team-working effectiveness and productivity. Reducing hidden areas also reduces the potential for confusion, misunderstanding, poor communication, etc., which all distract from and undermine team effectiveness.

Organisational culture and working atmosphere have a major influence on group members' preparedness to disclose their hidden selves. Most people fear judgment or vulnerability and therefore hold back hidden information, feelings, etc., that if moved into the open area (known by the group as well) would enhance mutual understanding, and thereby improve group awareness, enabling better individual performance and group effectiveness.

The extent to which an individual discloses personal feelings and information, and the issues which are disclosed, and to whom, must always be at the individual's own discretion. Some people are more keen and able than others to disclose. People should disclose at a pace and depth that they find personally comfortable. As with feedback, some people are more resilient than others—care needs to be taken to avoid causing emotional upset. Also as with soliciting feedback, the process of serious disclosure relates to the process of 'self-actualisation'.

Quadrant III shrinks in area as Quadrant I grows larger. We find it less necessary to hide or deny things we know or feel. In an atmosphere of growing mutual trust, there is less need for hiding pertinent thoughts or feelings. Relevant hidden information and feelings, etc., should be moved into the open area through the process of 'disclosure'. The aim should be to disclose and expose relevant information and feelings—hence the Johari Window terminology 'self-disclosure' and 'exposure process'—thereby increasing the open area. By telling others how we feel and other information about ourselves we reduce the hidden area, and increase the open area, which enables better understanding, cooperation, trust, team-working effectiveness and productivity. Reducing hidden areas also reduces the potential for confusion, misunderstanding, poor communication, etc., which all undermine team effectiveness.

During this learning process, Quadrant IV changes but we can assume that such changes occur even more slowly than shifts in Quadrant II. At any rate, Quadrant IV is undoubtedly far larger and more influential in an individual's relationships than the hypothetical sketch illustrates.

We have discussed earlier the various unknown factors that are intrinsic to this quadrant. There are various processes by which this information and knowledge can be uncovered. These can be prompted through self-discovery or observation by others, or in certain situations through collective or mutual discovery. If one does not wish that others know about this hidden factor, then counselling may be resorted to. By this method the information would be known only to the person who is counselling and not to the entire peer group.

Whether unknown, 'discovered' knowledge moves into the hidden, blind or open area depends on who discovers it and what they do with the knowledge, notably whether it is then given as feedback, or disclosed. Again as with disclosure and soliciting feedback, the process of self-discovery is a sensitive one. The extent and depth to which an individual is able to seek out discover their unknown feelings must always be at the individual's own discretion. Some people are more keen and able than others to do this.

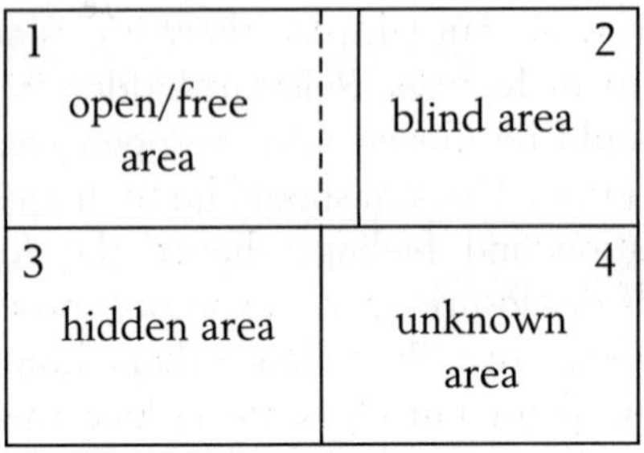

FIGURE 5 Johari Window 2

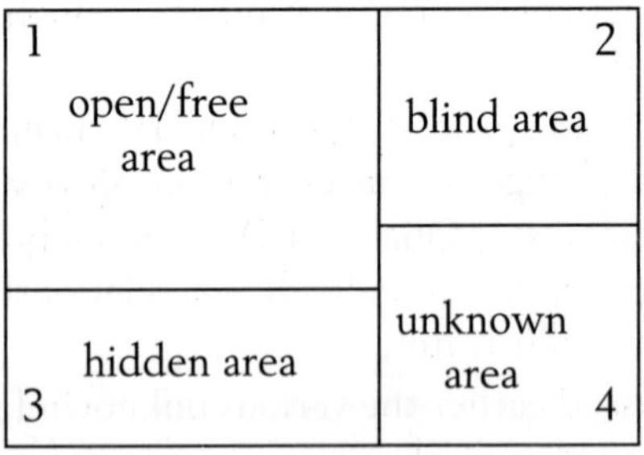

FIGURE 6 Johari Window 3

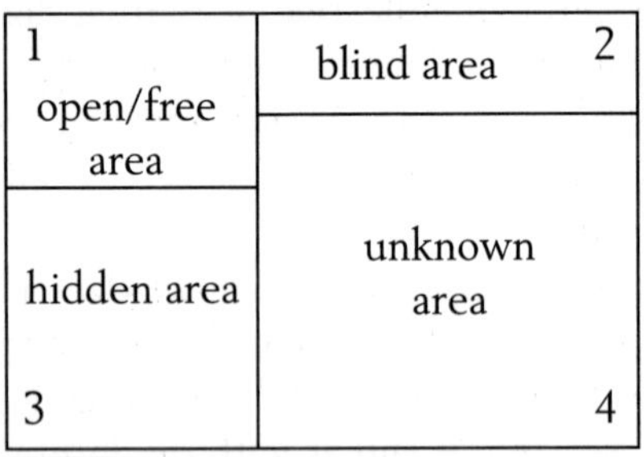

FIGURE 7 Johari Window 4

Uncovering 'hidden talents'—that is, unknown aptitudes and skills, not to be confused with developing the Johari 'hidden area'—is another aspect of developing the unknown area. Providing people with the opportunity to try new things, with no great pressure to succeed, is often a useful way to discover unknown abilities, and thereby reduce the unknown area.

Managers and leaders can help by creating an environment that encourages self-discovery, constructive observation, and feedback among team members. It is a widely accepted industrial fact that the majority of staff in any organisation are at any time working well within their potential. Creating a culture, climate, and expectation for self-discovery helps people use more of their potential and thereby to achieve more, and to contribute more to organisational performance.

However, a note of caution needs to be included. The unknown area could also include repressed or subconscious feelings rooted in formative events and traumatic past experiences, which can stay unknown for a lifetime. In a work or organisational context, the Johari Window should not be used to address issues of a clinical nature.

Other Variables Involving Interpersonal Communication

Besides feedback and disclosure, other variables also influence interpersonal aspects of communication. For example, lack of trust between colleagues leads to ineffective communication. People perceive only what they expect and want to perceive; the unexpected may not be perceived at all. Hence, differences in values and generation gaps are major variables. Status differential and incapability are areas of major concern. Having good interpersonal communication skills supports processes such as, selling, counselling, coaching, and mentoring and co-mentoring, which is mentoring in groups for conflict resolution. To achieve the goals set by the organisations and fostering effective interpersonal relationships, it is important that these variables are considered.

Patterns of Communication within an Organisation

Without effective communication, information is useless. Senior management of organisations need to establish effective paths of communication in order to ensure that necessary information reaches appropriate people. This information relates to both the operational policies, procedures and performances of the organisations. The organisational structure should facilitate a complete flow of information—upward, downward and across.

Information within an organisation flows through formal and informal channels. A free exchange of information helps the organisation respond rapidly to the changing market conditions, increase its efficiency and productivity, build employee morale, take full advantage of the knowledge of the workers, and serve the public.

Usually organisations use formal channels of communication. Information about policies and procedures originate with executives and flow down through the managers to the supervisors and finally to the lower-level employees. Many organisations formulate their own official communication policies that encourage regular, open communication, spell out responsibilities, and suggest means of achieving targets. Official communication between managers, supervisors, and workers occurs in four directions: upward, downward, lateral and diagonal.

Downward Communication

Organisations need to be structured in a way so as to maximise the benefits of the communication processes. Team structures are therefore very useful because they open up a multi-flow channel of communications.

Until the 1980's many large firms in America and Western Europe were characterised by top-down communications systems, which meant that communication flowed down the line, that is instructions were passed down the line, from the supervisors through the subordinates to the workers. However, in such situations individuals at the bottom end of the system have no or little scope for decision-making.

Downward communication provides direction and control. In this kind of communication, the information includes job plans, policies, and procedures. It is used to instruct employees so that managers can provide feedback regarding employee performance and instil in them the motivation to achieve the organisation's goals. This type of communication can take the form of a written directive, face-to-face conversations, a public address system, bulletin boards and a company's in-house journals and newsletters.

Certain obstacles can hamper downward communication leading to distortion. Due to the long chain of people through which the message is transmitted, there are all chances of the message being distorted. For example, if the CEO wants to change the accounting procedure then he/she would not send a memo directly to the staff. Instead, the message would be sent from the office of the President to the Controller of Finance to the Accounting Manager, who in turn would send it to his/her subordinates until the message reaches the affected employees. Nevertheless, in this process due to a long line of communication the chances of the message being distorted are greater than otherwise.

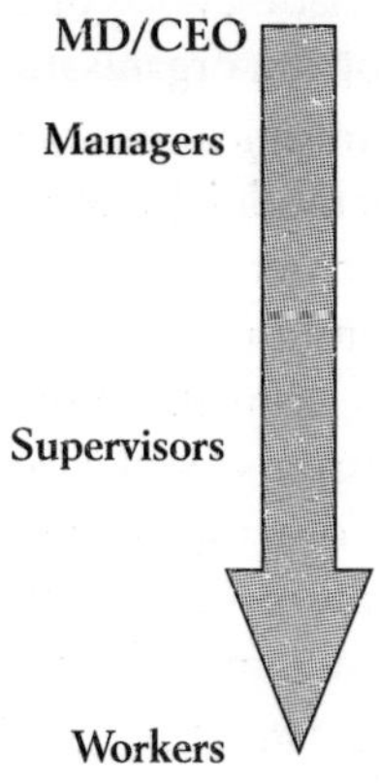

FIGURE 8 Downward Communication

To overcome such problems and improve communication, nowadays large organisations are resorting to the formation of smaller operating units and work teams. The management speaks directly to the team leaders keeping in mind that the transmission of the correct message should reach the lowermost rung at the operating level, speeding up the entire process as well as. Instead of hoarding information at the top, today's management recognises the fact that workers should be kept informed about how the company is doing and the projects that the company is plannings planning.

Upward Communication

Messages that move up the hierarchy from the subordinate to the supervisor constitute upward communication. Upward communication involves feedback of ideas from lower down in the organisation to higher levels. This sort of communication flow is important in the consultation of employees, and enables managers to draw on good ideas from those working at grassroots levels in an organisation.

Research has shown that upward communication is often subject to distortion because subordinates withhold or distort information that makes them look bad. This form of information travel facilitates and ensures that the board of directors and senior management are made aware of the business risks and the operating performance of the organisation.

Earlier, upward communication was not used much in a hierarchical management model. However, since we now line in the 'flattened' world, management philosophy has changed in favour of upward flow of communication. Channels for upward flow include phone messages, e-mails, memos, reports, department meetings, suggestion systems, and grievance committees. It is interesting to note that downward communication tends to be expanded in terms of interpretation and impact, while upward information is compiled, examined, reduced, and passed on.

A number of obstacles can interrupt the upward movement of information. Employees who distrust their superiors are likely to communicate less with them. The cause could be that they have been tricked, manipulated, criticised, or treated unfairly. This may result in the management not knowing the exact happenings in the shop-floors. It is likely that a supervisor may not pass a good suggestion from a worker thinking that the worker may get all the credit or get promoted thus exposing his inefficiency in handling the department. The resulting consequences may thus harm the efficiency of the team and future of organisation.

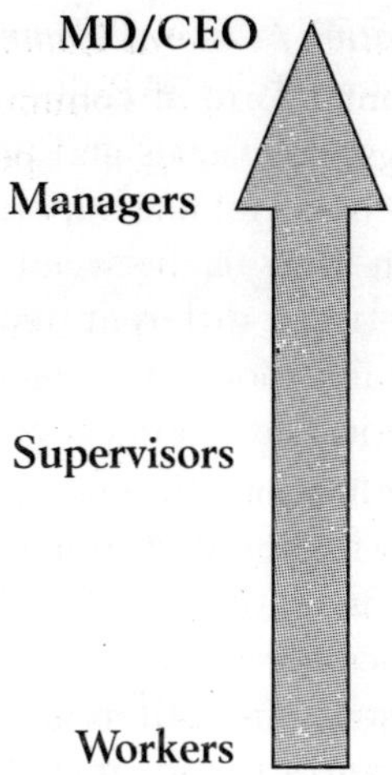

FIGURE 9 Upward Communication

To improve the upward flow of communication, organisations should create a climate and an environment that helps junior employees communicate freely. The responsibility for a free flow of upward communication largely rests with the superiors. Realising the need and importance of this form of communication, nowadays, some companies are taking the following steps: a. hiring communication coaches to train their employees, b. asking employees to report customer complaints, c. encouraging regular meetings with the staff, d. ensuring a non-threatening environment for staff and e. offering incentive programmes which encourages employees to collect and share valuable feedback. They are also setting up hotlines for anonymous feedbacks and recruiting 'ombudsmen' (mediators who hear employees' complaints), to investigate and resolve problems impartially and objectively.

Thus, both the upward and the downward flow of information constitute vertical communication that is an internal system of communication in organisations.

Horizontal Communication / Lateral Communication

In the lateral or horizontal form of communication, information flows or travels amongst colleagues and peers at the same level in the organisation such as training supervisors or maintenance engineers. Information flow is between people of the same department, or it is between different departments. This is also known as 'peer communication'. It is far more informal, social, and voluntary than vertical communication.

It facilitates coordination among interdependent units. Examples of this kind of communication include, sales managers for different regions circulating details of potential customers to each other and allocating work based on customer location; or the accounting staff in different departments sharing information to help prepare the annual budget. Horizontal/ lateral communication plays a major role in matrix designs or in committees that have representatives from several departments. The channels usually used for this type of communication are personal contacts, e-mails, telephone calls, memos, voice mails, and meetings. Traditional organisations had very few horizontal channels for communication since they largely followed the top-down approach.

The world today has changed from a hierarchical world of kings and queens to a 'flattened' world of democracy, knowledge and computers. From a vertical world of clearly defined class hierarchies the world is now becoming horizontal. Thomas L. Friedman (2005) notes, 'The world is moving from a vertical, command and control system to a more horizontal, connect and collaborate system'. He asserts that this has created a 'flat-world platform' that has empowered and enabled individuals and small groups to go global. What it really means is that all knowledge centres on this planet are being connected through a global network to bring in an era of prosperity, innovation, and collaboration between companies, communities and individuals. As mentioned earlier, Manuel Castells calls this 'network society'—connected by the Internet, computers, telephones, cell phones, video-conferencing, voice-mail and other communication technologies.

This change since 1995 is mainly because of the wide use of personal computers, fibre optic cable technology for digitisation of information and its conveyance around the world at negligible cost and the workflow software. All these factors have contributed substantially to create a 'flat-world platform'. Horizontal communication plays a key role in this process.

Now with flattened hierarchies, and team-based management, the companies have rediscovered that when employees combine their knowledge with that of other employees, it promotes understanding and they can do their jobs more efficiently.

However, poor communication skills, ego involvement, prejudice, and turf wars are some of the unavoidable obstacles in this type of communication. Some employees resist sharing information as they feel that it would endanger their status and reduce their chances of getting a promotion. Competition within departments or an uneven reward system may also prevent the workers from sharing information.

To improve this type of communication, the onus is on both the management as well as the employees. Therefore, the companies are; a. training their employees in teamwork and communication skills, b. establishing reward system based on team achievement rather than individual achievement, and c. encouraging full participation in team functions. On the part of the employees, it is their responsibility to voice their opinions and at the same time be sensitive and tolerant to other people's opinions; both together can promote understanding and goodwill in any organisation to increase its productivity and efficiency.

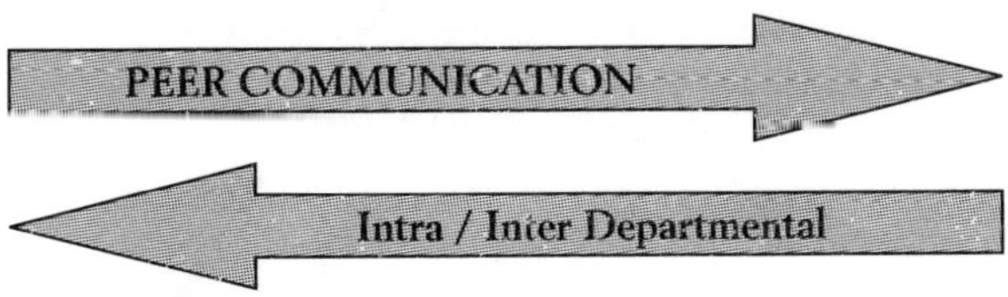

FIGURE 10 Horizontal Communication

Diagonal Communication

Diagonal communication is quite uncommon and involves interdepartmental communication by people at different levels and different hierarchies. This kind of communication involves people who have no direct reporting relationships with one another and therefore information can be exchanged speedily for the sake of efficiency. The 'criss-cross' of information tkat takes place through the formal channels depends on the interdependence among various departments. If the business requires coordinated action, then the communication is frequent and intense. However, if each department acts independently, official horizontal communication becomes minimal. A good example would be a project team drawn from different grades and departments.

However, there are potential drawbacks in this system. Since such communication involves communicating outside of the department, it can cause internal friction or misunderstanding. Secondly, it undermines the authority of a boss or a manager by making promises or commitments that involve the entire department or unit.

If one has to indulge in diagonal communication, then permission must be obained from the supervisor to refrain from making any commitments beyond one's authority; and inform the direct supervisor of any significant result and about important developments in interdepartmental activities.

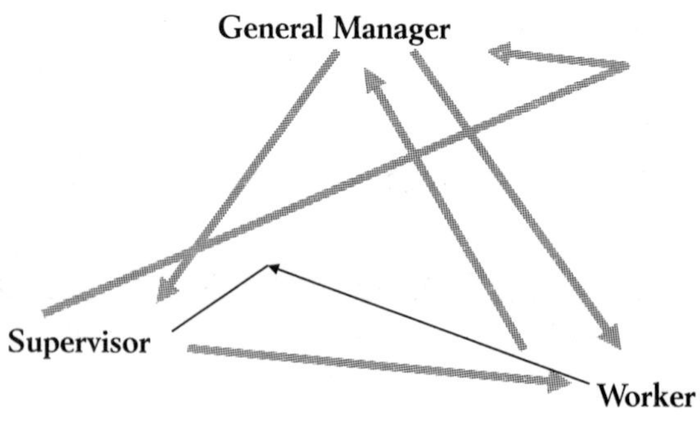

FIGURE 11 Diagonal Communication

Grapevine Communication

The flow of information and communication in various directions that we have just discussed constitutes the formal way of communicating in an organisation. An informal network, unsanctioned yet supplementing the official channel, exists within an organisation, which is known as 'grapevine'.

Grapevine is the informal transmission of information, gossip or rumour from person to person. Donald S. Simmons (1985), states that 'the network helps employees make sense of the world around them and consequently provides a release from emotional stress and all informal information is undocumented.' Keith Davis (1976) discovered in his study that organisational grapevine is an expression of healthy human motivation to communicate, 'In fact, if employees are so uninterested in their work that they do not engage in shoptalk about it, they are probably maladjusted,' say Ralph L. Rosnow and Gary Alan Fine (1976).

Employee communication typically consists of a newsletter, an occasional employee meeting, and stacks of memos with numbing operational details that few employees read and fewer still comprehend. The typical company newsletter, according to the majority of employees, is outdated, boring, self-serving for the management that is hardly read at all. The absence of effective and informative employee communication leaves the field open for anyone to say anything and voice one's opinion to start grapevine communication.

However, Keith Davis notes that grapevine is a natural part of a company's total communication system. It is a significant force within the work group, helping to build teamwork to motivate people, and create corporate identity. It is an informal passing of information through the organisation. It does not necessarily follow the formal structure of an organisation and can bypass individuals without restraint. It can be more direct and faster than the formal channels of information since the information is not screened or controlled. Interestingly, the grapevine is equally active both in management and workers.

Reasons for its Existence

The grapevine exists in organisations for many reasons. Some of them are listed below:

1. Grapevine communication, being personal and flexible can carry and spread useful information in the organisation with amazing speed. It supplements the formal channels.
2. It provides people with an outlet for their imaginations and apprehensions as well. It also helps satisfy a natural desire to know what is really going on and gives employees a sense of belonging.
3. As an early warning system, gossip allows people to think through in advance what they will do if the rumours become the awful truth. Subordinates may get an idea of what the boss is wrestling with and come up with always that may help the situation.
4. It is also capable of penetrating even the tightest security because it cuts across organisational lines and deals directly with people in the know. Bosses who choose not to pay attention to the grapevine have less credible information than those who do.

Pradip Khandwalla (1977) states that it exists because there is excessive structuring of formal workflows and excessive channelling of information flow. It becomes stifling for the employees who require some outlet to air their own views and opinions. They also seem to be fed by personal apprehension, wish fulfilment, retaliation, and gossip (Frederick Koenig, 1985). Surprisingly, most researchers have found that most grapevine information is either true or has within it a kernel of truth. The corporate culture becomes defined by the grapevine rather than by visionary design.

Spread of Grapevine

Within the organisation, many communication chains exist. The chain used by formal communication may be very rigid, following the chain of command or authority. However, the chain used by the grapevine tends to be very flexible. According to Keith Davis the following four chains/structures appear to dominate the grapevine network:

1. **The Single Strand Chain :** This is a simple concept to follow, A tells B, who tells C, who tells D and so on. Each person passes the information on to the next person. The longer the strand, more the distortion and filtering affecting the information being passed until the last person in the chain may find the information unrecognisable from the original message. Most inaccuracies occur in this chain.

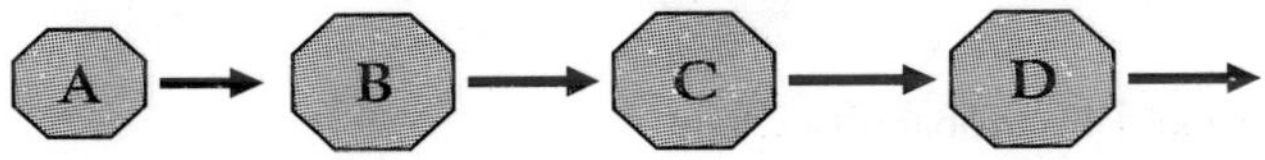

FIGURE 12 Single Strand Chain

2. **The Gossip Chain:** In this illustration, A simply tells everyone with whom he/she comes in contact with. Single individuals spread the news. Nevertheless, this pattern is considered to be somewhat slow in moving the information.

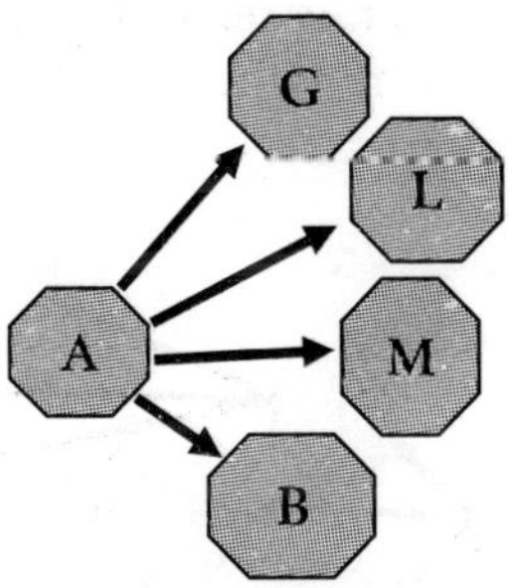

FIGURE 13 Gossip Chain

3. **The Probability Chain:** In this case A makes random contact with say F and C and passes on the information. They in turn randomly contact others in accordance with laws of probability. Some hear the information and some don't. In this structure, there is no definite pattern of communication. Information is randomly passed along to anyone willing to listen. The person who communicates in this manner might be a very outgoing and talkative.

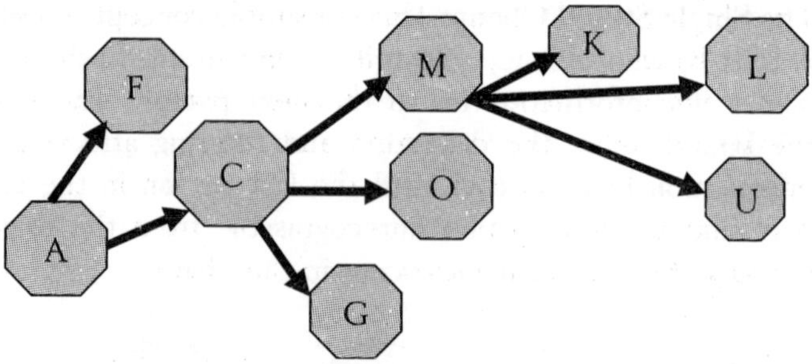

FIGURE 14 Probability Chain

5. **The Cluster Chain:** The most predominant pattern is the cluster pattern. Here A passes on information to contacts, B and F, who may work with A. They may convey this information to two or three other persons with whom they usually have close contact. Selectivity is the basis for this pattern. In any organisation, generally, individuals will feel more comfortable with some fellow employees than with others and therefore information is relayed to those in their informal social groups. This flow results in information missing some individuals completely.

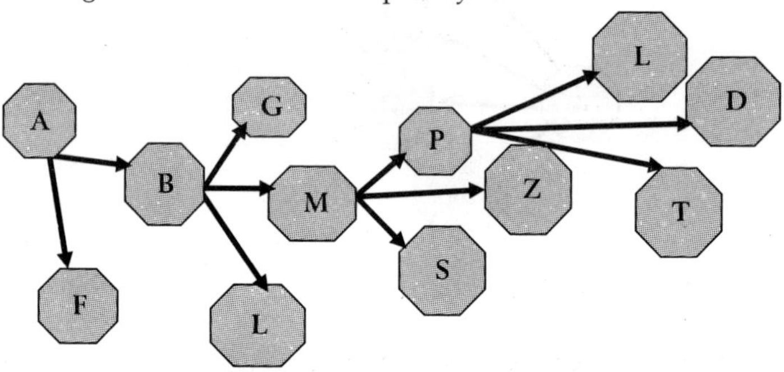

FIGURE 15 Cluster Chain

Limitations of Grapevine

Though grapevine exists in every organisation, it has serious limitations. First, it is impossible to predict the direction, speed, accuracy, or final content of a message carried by grapevine.

Secondly, in the process of transmission the message may get abbreviated, magnified, restructured, elaborated, or generally distorted. Thirdly, the grapevine respects nobody and may ascribe the worst possible motives to the noblest of people. It may spread baseless and distorted information that may prove harmful to individuals.

As the grapevine information lacks careful drafting it is generally incomplete. Therefore, information is likely to get misinterpreted.

Members of the grapevine may form groups and cliques and use the information for their own benefits. These cliques can lead to frictions and conflicts thereby defeating the very purpose of having an informal communication system.

Since swiftness of transmission is the hallmark of grapevine, a rumour may spread like lightning causing serious damage before the management becomes aware of it and can take any damage control measures.

Positive Aspects of Grapevine

Even though management does not always view grapevine favourably, it has several positive aspects.

One major advantage of the grapevine is that it is a release mechanism for stress. Bottled-up feelings prove to have negative side effects for individuals and the grapevine helps to ease this type of situation.

We know individuals like and need to talk about their work. It is an important part of one's life, and in talking about work, the grapevine gives employees the opportunity to convert official company policies into their own language or jargon. In doing this, individuals are better able to understand the policies and are better able to cope with their work environment

This open and informal communication also enables employees to have empathy for those who are stressed outside of the work place. As stronger personal bonds occur among workers, a greater spirit of teamwork exists within the organisation.

As grapevine transfers information speedily, it enables individuals to think in advance, prepare for, and think through the goal changes and goal adjustments of the management before it makes any formal statements. This increases the contributions made by employees.

The grapevine also helps employees to remain efficient by quickly spreading the news of disciplinary actions. If tardiness is a problem and one person is given a day off without pay, will management be able to remind everyone immediately of the company policy? Probably not. Will a memo from the personnel department reach everyone that same day? That is not likely to happen either. However, will the grapevine make sure everyone is at work on time the next day? Oh, yes!

Additionally, the grapevine is a good indicator of health, morale, trends, and productivity. The grapevine reveals issues and problems being discussed by the employees and the effect of policies and procedures upon which the employees can be evaluated.

The grapevine is also a means of communication that a manager can use to increase efficiency. Managers should have some means of tapping into the grapevine. Using this method, desired information can be circulated quickly to a large group of subordinates.

Control of the grapevine is an understated responsibility of the manager. While not all the information passing through it is initiated by the management, nevertheless, the responsibility for the accuracy of information ultimately rests on the management.

Managing Grapevine Effectively

No one can deny the existence of grapevine in any work place. The issue therefore which needs to be addressed is how managers can deal effectively with the grapevine? Primarily, managers should accept the fact and decide how they can use it to their own benefit. Vanessa Arnold (1983) contends, 'Managers interested in creating effective organisational communication will use information from the grapevine to improve communication throughout the firm.'

Managers certainly need special skills to deal with grapevine. They must realise that it can neither be suppressed nor can it ever die. Therefore, instead of curbing its growth, it is much better to nurture and cultivate it. It is essential that the manager finds out the 'grapevine facts' and understand how they work. The real value of grapevine should be in revealing to management those issues that generate from the grass roots and use it for the benefit of the organisation.

Since grapevine activity increases during times of uncertainty, management must provide information through the formal system of communication about key issues and events that affect employees. Most importantly, announcement of important information should be made well in advance of the release date so that the official announcement can create enthusiasm and interest.

Management should supply employees with a steady flow of accurate, timely information; so that the potential damage caused by the grapevine can be minimised. Any attempt to soften or distort a rumour to make things look good is not a good way to deal with the rumour. The longer a rumour circulates the more difficult it is to control. The grapevine can be controlled with the release of prompt, clear, and accurate information on the issues important to the employees. Full facts must be presented. Formal communication lines must be kept open and the process should be made as short as possible. Direct memos, large group announcements, and intercom systems should be used. If employees perceive that management is providing them with facts, they will be less anxious and less emotional when rumours are heard.

The grapevine can be used to see how a new idea is received. A bit of information may be dropped on the grapevine in order to test the possible reaction to a proposed decision. If feedback through grapevine indicates an unfavourable reaction, management can reconsider the idea or alter it to lessen employee resistance. If the new idea is incorporated, management is thus forewarned of problems so as to be prepared with new programmes to help overcome anxiety and misperceptions. In short, feelings and possible effects can be sensed early and the management can adopt corrective measures. John Kotter (1985), a Harvard Business

School professor gives an example of a manager he knows who uses the grapevine to give new ideas a 'trial-run' before spending a great deal of time and money. 'He knows who in the office has the longest tongue,' explains Kotter. He then casually mentions this new idea to the employee and waits for the word to spread. In no time, responses find their way back to his secretary, who gives him a full report. Feedback is very important, and if it is positive, he goes ahead with the new plan. If the feedback is negative, it is back to the drawing board to rethink the idea. Thus, grapevine can be used to feel and judge the pulse of the employees.

Bill Hunter (1984) says, writes that some organisations create a rumour hotline or rumour control office. When an employee hears a rumour he can call the rumour office to check it out. By providing this service, bad rumours can be replaced with good rumours. It is suggested by Peter J. Nofel (1985), that a training program be conducted for employees on the nature of rumours so that the employees can distinguish between good and bad rumours.

To conclude, it may be said that employee communication should be carefully strategised like various advertising and marketing programs by the management at the highest level. Above all, employee communication should be consistent in its message to minimise confusion and to maximise the impact. If employees hear one thing from one source and something contradictory from another source, they cannot understand exactly what to believe, but it leaves them with the impression that the management is also confused, not knowing what exactly it wants (and sometimes they are right!). Consistency builds familiarity and confidence in the validity of communications. It also constantly reinforces the message, implants it deeper into the culture. Fear of the unknown, of being left out, is what drives employees who feel 'like a mushroom' to turn to the grapevine as their primary source of information in a gaming company. Therefore, it is important to keep the employees 'in the loop' so that it makes them feel more like insiders, a part of an inner circle. It makes them feel important and needed. These are basic human motivations, nuances of human relationships and communication present in all cultures that has to be strictly maintained in any organisation.

Activities

1. Write a note on each of the following.
   - the manner in which an employee learns of the goings on in the organisation
   - the kind of information that flows through the formal channels
   - the kind of information that flows through the informal channels
   - the kind of information that flows through the grapevine
2. Explain with the help of examples how the grapevine is an asset to any organisation.
3. Certain situations given below show how information spreads through the grapevine. Read each of the following and identify the type of grapevine through which the message was transmitted.
   - A group of students have organised a picnic to Kabirwad. The class representative has told Reena to spread the message to whoever she meets.
   - The head of the department asks a faculty member (A) to pass on the message of a meeting to be held on the 4 March 2010. A passes the message to B, B to C, C to D till all the members are informed.
   - John wants to hold a party for his best friend Seema on successfully clearing her MBA examinations. He asks Meena to convey this message to two of their friends, Suresh and Rakesh. Each of these two in turn conveys the message to two more friends. This chain continues until all the 25 friends are informed.
   - A passes the information on the date of commencement of final examinations to F and C. They in turn randomly contact others and pass on the message.

REFERENCES

Arnold, Dean Venessa. 1983. Harvesting Your Employee Grapevine: With Insight You Can Transform the Rumor Mill into a Valuable Communication Network. *Management World*. 12:28.

Castells, Manuel. 1996. The Information Age: Economy, Society and Culture. Vol. 1 of *The Rise of the Network Society*. Oxford: Blackwell Publishers.

Davis, Keith. 1969. Grapevine Communication among Lower and Middle Managers. *Personnel Journal* Apr.:272.

Friedman, Thomas L. 2005. *The World is Flat: A Brief History of the Twenty-first Century*. New York: Farrar, Straus and Giroux.

Guffey, Mary Ellen. 2000. *Business Communication: Process and Product*. Cincinnati: Thomson South-Western.

Khandwalla, Pradip N. 1977. *Design of Organizations*. New York: Harcourt.

Koenig, Fredrick. 1985. *Rumor in the Marketplace: The Social Psychology of Commercial Hearsay*. Dover, MA: Auburn House.

Kotter, John. 1985. *Power and Influence: Beyond Formal Authority*. New York: Free Press.

Luft, Joseph. 1969. *Of Human Interaction*. Paolo Alto: National Press.

Luthans, Fred. 1992. *Organizational Behavior*. New York: McGraw Hill.

Nofel, Peter J. 1985. Cultivating the Office Grapevine. *Modern Office Technology* 30:117.

Rosnow, Ralph L. and Gary Alan Fine. 1976. *Rumor and Gossip: The Social Psychology of Hearsay*. New York: Elsevier.

Simmons, Donald S. 1985. The Nature of Organizational Grapevine. *Supervisory Management* Nov.:39.

Chapter 3

E-mail Communication

Context

Globalisation, privatisation and liberalisation are the three main driving forces that have changed the economic, political and social structures of the world. All these processes depend heavily on communication between individuals, communities, companies and nations. Consequently, a new set of tools have been developed with the help of information technology to make this communication easy, fast, safe and economical.

Globalisation has changed the world so much that the world is now perceived to be a 'flat' one in which there is a free flow of information and communication between individuals, corporations and even nations for economic and political purposes. Thomas L. Friedman (2005) notes,

> 'What the flattening of the world means is that we are now connecting all the knowledge centres on the planet into a single global network, which—if politics and terrorism do not get in the way—could usher in an amazing era of prosperity, innovation, and collaboration by companies, communities and individuals.'

This has happened because of the availability of personal computers in offices and homes, fibre optic cable technology for digitisation of information and its conveyance around the globe at no cost, and workflow software like that of Dell Computers manufactured in multinational locations and sold around the globe through the electronic business (e-business) mode.

Analysing these networks, Manuel Castells in his ground-breaking book *The Rise of Network Society* (1996) observes that there are three kinds of networks operating in the world today: business, technological and, social and cultural. Besides this, there are also networked forms of global governance. All these networks have developed a culture of communication that makes the twenty-first century the century of communication. Today we live in a culture of communication for the sake of communication. It is an open-ended network of cultural meanings that not only coexist, but interact and modify each other on the basis of this exchange.

This culture of the network society is a culture of protocols of communication between all cultures in the world. It has developed on the basis of the common belief in the power of networking and of synergy. It is a process rather than a product and is unified by the common belief in the use value of sharing. This culture promotes and supports electronic business.

E-BUSINESS

E-business is the business of buying and selling goods, commodities and services through the electronic mode. It also includes servicing customers, collaborating with business partners in diverse global locations, and conducting electronic transactions within an organisation. Hence, it is all about time cycle, speed, globalisation, enhanced productivity, reaching new customers and sharing knowledge across institutions for competitive advantage. Though it depends heavily on technology and is addressed by computer experts, marketing research experts and experts on consumer behaviour and communication occupy the centre-space in this business.

There are three kinds of e-business transactions:

a. business-to-business (when transaction takes place between one business and another business);
b. business to consumer and
c. intra-business (when transactions take place within an organisation).

All these three kinds of businesses, however, need fast, easy, safe and low-cost communication that can be conducted easily through the Internet.

Similarly, advertising is another business which targets potential buyers through electronic messages using Internet, radio, television, cell phones, etc. Companies like Google, Yahoo, Hotmail, Rediffmail, Indiatimes, etc. generate huge revenues through this mode, which can be updated any time at a minimal cost. It can reach a large number of potential buyers, all over the world cheaply and effectively using the convergence of text, audio, graphics, and animation. The products can be made interactive and targeted to specific interest groups and individuals.

E-business also covers online services like cyber banking, stock trading, travel and tourism, real estate, job seeking and job giving, electronic catalogues and electronic payment systems. Cyber shopping, cyber publishing, etc. are forms of e-business or commerce. All these businesses depend heavily on electronic communication, mostly done through electronic mail, a system for sending and receiving messages electronically over a computer network, as between personal computers. The term e-mail is also used for a message or messages sent or received by such a system.

E-MAIL

Electronic mail, popularly known as e-mail, is electronic, global and interactive. It is a combination of many communication technologies such as television, telephone, publishing and web surfing. Besides being fast, it can carry pictures, videos and audio materials, publish both text and hypertext in cyberspace and be stored on the web. E-mails are easily accessible anytime and anywhere in the world. Audio and video clips easily fit into this format and can be sent as an attachment or within the message. These messages can be notes typed on the keyboard of a computer or electronic files containing photographs, audio or video materials stored in the computer or on a compact disc.

Technically speaking, e-mail is a method of communication whereby an individual or a company uses a computer or some other electronic device (like a cell phone) to compose and send a message to another individual or a group of individuals. Messages may be sent through computer systems linked by a network or through modems using telephone lines. E-mails may also be sent through wireless transmissions as in the case of BlackBerry cell phones. They can be sent to one user at a time or broadcast to several users at the same time and usually take only a few minutes to arrive at their destination. Hence, e-mail is typically used to bypass regular postal service delivery (often referred to as snail mail) and to speed communication.

Every e-mail user has a unique address, such as john@gmail.com or disha02@rediffmail.com. Companies, institutions and governments create addresses for their employees for transacting business related to their work and for easy identification.

Writing an E-mail

As an e-mail is a mail or a letter sent electronically, unlike a letter which is written on paper, put into an envelope and then sent through a post office or a courier, it is sent through a mail server electronically, read on the computer screen and is generally replied to immediately by clicking the reply button. Once it has been typed on screen, it is proof-read for errors or omissions and then sent as a reply to the sender of the letter. It should therefore be written like a letter and not like a telegraph or an SMS (short message service) which have space constraints.

E-mail is fast, flexible and reliable, though not always secure. Fully computerised companies use it extensively both for internal and external communication. It is used for all kinds of business communication including business inquiries, confirming orders, sending press releases, announcing sales promotions, explaining price changes and updating scripts, besides a host of other purposes.

FORMATTING AN E-MAIL

It is important to format e-mails properly to ensure that it is received and read by the person it is sent to. If the receiver is unable to read the e-mail a failure in communication occurs resulting in loss of business. Therefore, a set format must be followed in sending e-mail messages.

E-mails consist of the following two major sections.

- Header—structured into fields such as summary, sender, receiver and other information about the e-mail
- Body—the message itself as unstructured text; sometimes containing a signature block at the end

Header

Each message has one header, which is structured into fields. The message header usually includes at least the following fields.

- From: the e-mail address and optionally the name of the sender
- To: the e-mail address[es] and optionally name[s] of the message's recipient[s]
- Subject: a title for the message
- Date: the local time and date when the message was written

Other common header fields include:

- Cc: carbon copy
- Bcc: blind carbon copy

The most popular format for e-mail is the Microsoft Internet format available in text and HTML formats:

While some transmission systems provide links only within a company's particular e-mail system, the other systems provide e mail users the facility to access various systems around the world. In order to send an e-mail message, each party must have an e-mail address. The address is composed of an identifying name, an @ sign, the name of the file server where the account is located and a domain name. Typical domain names are .com (commercial), .gov (government), .edu (schools), and .org (organisation). An example of an e-mail address would be amarsingh@amd.com. In order to send a message outside the company e-mail system, the complete address must be used.

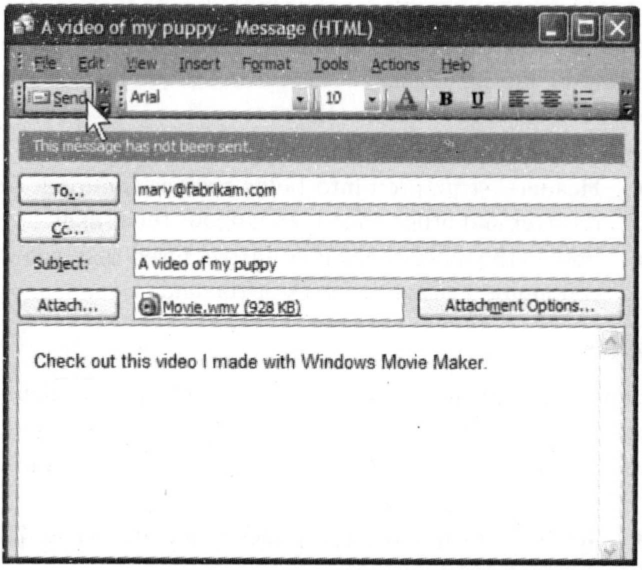

Organising E-mail

When e-mail messages arrive, the reader can reply, forward or delete them. The messages can be stored either on the web through such websites as www.gmail.com or www.hotmail.com or can be put in the Inboxes of Outlook Express and other such services. E-mail systems also have filters to organise incoming messages and folders to organise messages that need to be stored. In such cases the reader transfers the message to the appropriate folder clearing the inbox of the message and providing a logical way of locating a message either by sender or by topic.

Address book: Most electronic mail systems offer an address book feature, which provide a place to store e-mail addresses. As these addresses are often complex and difficult to remember, they can be easily stored in the address book, which can also be used to develop mailing lists. For example, if six friends frequently communicate, a user might list all their addresses in a 'folder' in the address book with a name such as 'My Friends'. Then the user could quickly send a message to all six friends at one time by addressing the message to 'My Friends' rather than to each individual user. Similar lists could be developed for your business partners, suppliers, distributors or customers.

Attachments: E-mail users can send documents by using the attachment feature. This allows the user to specify where an electronic file—such as a text document, a spreadsheet, or a graphics presentation—is located. It also allows the user to send a copy by e-mail. Attachments can be sent to a list of people in one e-mail message. This feature has greatly enhanced the ability of people to bridge distances and to work together. For example, if two people are planning a presentation at a conference, they can attach outlines of the presentation as well as slides of the actual presentation and transmit them for revision or review.

Photographs and audio-files containing speech or songs can be attached to e-mail messages or through a 'link' in the message. However, multimedia files including photos, take a long time to send as they are large files. Digital cameras and scanners have made it easier to send photographs via e-mail.

Plain text and HTML: E-mails are sent or received both in plain text and HTML formats. While text format is more popular as it can easily be read even on low-end computer systems, HTML has more aesthetic appeal. Moreover, this format allows in-line links and transfer of audio-video files and images easily. It is easier to set apart previous messages in block quotes, wrap naturally on any display, and emphasise by underlining or italicising or even changing font style. However, HTML e-mails are not as safe as text messages because they can easily be hacked and are bitten by 'web bugs'. HTML e-mail messages often include an automatically-generated plain text copy as well. 'Phishing' or luring of an Internet user to reveal personal details (like passwords and credit card information) on a fake web page or e-mail form pretending to come from a legitimate company (like their bank) can happen easily on HTML format.

Deleting a message: After reading an incoming e-mail message, if the reader decides that he/she doesn't need the message, it can be deleted immediately. However, many systems keep the deleted messages in a trash folder till such a file is deleted permanently.

Forwarding a message: If the reader decides to send a received message to a third party, it may be done by choosing the 'Forward' option on message itself. The receiver, in turn, can easily forward the message either to an individual or a list of individuals.

Implementing e-mail policies: In order to keep a track of official correspondence, many organisations have implemented e-mail policies in their offices. These policies allow the employers to review and monitor the incoming and outgoing mails through their computer systems. Courts uphold the right of corporations to review the e-mail of employees who use company resources such as hardware, software, and/or company time to compose and send e-mail messages. In the opinion of law, a company has the right to read the e-mail of employees, particularly, if such companies have an e-mail policy in place.

Junk mail or spam: These are unwanted e-mails, usually of commercial nature sent out in bulk. They come into the inbox in the form of chain letters, unsolicited advertisements, fake warnings about viruses or files, and other non-business information. Such e-mails should not be opened and read as they are likely to corrupt our files or hanging the system.

Replying to a message: Replying to an e-mail is very easy. If the reader wishes to respond to an e-mail message, he/she can do so by clicking the 'reply' button without retyping the e-mail address of the sender. However, one should be careful in replying when a common e-mail has been sent to a list so as to reply only to the sender and not all the recipients. For example, a conference coordinator sends a reminder message to a list of 500 people who will be attending a conference. One of the respondents has a question about whether her registration has arrived and replies to the message using the 'reply' button. Since the original message was sent to a list, it is quite possible that the reply may be sent to all the 500 people on the list. This will result in the violation of 'netiquette,' discussed below. Be careful to select the 'reply to sender' option in such cases.

NETIQUETTE

Netiquette is Internet etiquette and courtesy to be kept in mind when using shared services and mailing lists on the Internet. Using these rules for sending and receiving e-mails helps us to be socially responsible members of the community of Internet users or 'netizens'.

Netiquette, therefore, is a set of socially acceptable rules of behaviour on the Internet. They help us to behave correctly and acceptably on the net just as rules of social etiquette do in society. For example, interrupting a speaker, and not introducing people you are with to others are examples of bad etiquette. Similarly, 'flaming' (sending an immediate, angry overreaction to an e-mail), 'shouting' (typing a message in capital letters), or sending a personal message to an entire list are violations of netiquette.

Some Important Points to Remember

- Always use the subject line as most organisations filter their mails keeping in mind the position/department that the mail is addressed to. In case it is difficult or not possible, use a subject line that will get the attention of the concerned person.
- Mention the name of the concerned person while starting your covering letter. If not, you can start with 'Sir' or 'Madam'.
- Keep the content of your mail crisp and to the point. Avoid using general addresses such as 'To whomsoever it may concern', or 'Kind Attention'.
- Avoid 'shouting' by using capital letters where not required (For example: NEVER WRITE A FULL LETTER IN CAPITALS).

- Do not use the chat mode, SMS language or short forms of any kind in an official mail transacting some serious business like applying for a job.
- Always use formal language, correct grammar, punctuation and sentence construction. Also, close your covering letter properly. (For example by saying, 'Thanks and regards' before signing off.)
- In business letters, do not use any smilies or other images, icons or symbols.
- When sending an application through e-mail, write a short paragraph about why you are right for the job and mention that you have attached your CV for reference. Do not forget to mention your telephone number in the e-mail even if you have already mentioned it in your CV.
- When attaching a document, ensure that the file is named correctly. For example, a file called 'Copy_CV_' in the e-mail may be renamed 'CV' so that is is easy for the recipient to identify the file.
- If the sender has asked you to follow a format, do follow it otherwise your message may not be read at all. Some people may ask for a word file and some may specifically ask you not to send attachments.
- Ensure that you do not send a CC to anyone else but the concerned person. Do not forward or send your CV to many people in a single e-mail.
- Do not use fancy user IDs or e-mail addresses for official purposes. Companies, institutions, government agencies, etc. generally use the names of their employees as their user names. In case you are unable to use your name, keep it as close to your name as possible, simple and easy to remember.
- Before you send your job application through e-mail, do a virus scan of your attachments. This is to ensure that your future employer does not have to remove the virus before reading the message. In such a case your mail may not be read at all.

Guidelines for Business E-mails

- One should not be casual and careless in using language in official e-mails. Therefore avoid using unnecessary abbreviations and words that are not in common use.
- Be careful about sending a copy through 'CC', particularly when you are sending sensitive information.
- While replying to an e-mail, avoid 'composing' a new message because it will break the 'thread of the conversation', and the receiver will have to look into his files for reference.
- If you have to respond to several questions or points, reply by answering under each question. You may even use a different font colour for the answers making your answers standout grabbing the attention of the recipient immediately.
- Send a 'CC' only to those who need it and not to everyone on your mailing list.
- As far as possible, reply to the sender immediately after receiving an e-mail so the recipient would know that you have received his/her e-mail. However, if you need some time to prepare a formal reply, do inform the sender that you have received the message and would reply soon in detail.
- Never use your official e-mail for personal correspondence as your mails are likely to be monitored.
- E-mail conversations have to be clear and there should be no scope for misunderstandings. So, we should be careful about the language we use and be polite.
- Large number of incoming e-mails are a matter of concern for most companies. Using the priority rating systems, some companies flag them for immediate response. Others choose a concise subject line that clearly defines the message. It is therefore recommended that either of the two systems be used for deciding the priority of the message and the time taken to respond.
- When you forward an e-mail, delete all of the other addresses that appear in the body of the message (at the

top) as no one wants to scroll through 200 e-mail addresses to read his/her e-mail.

- When you send an e-mail to more than one person, you can also use the BCC: (blind carbon copy) option to ensure that the recipent gets due attention.
- Do not forward chain e-mails to a business address.

How does an e-mail work?

The following diagram will help explain the typical sequence of events in e-mail system. A messge is first composed using a computer or Mail User Agent (MUA). After the e-mail address of the recipient is keyed in and the 'send' button is clicked, the message is sent instantaneously.

1. The sender's MUA formats the message in Internet e-mail format and uses the Simple Mail Transfer Protocol (SMTP) to send the message to the local Mail Transfer Agent (MTA), in this case *smtp.rec.org*, run by the recipient's Internet Service Protocol (ISP).
2. The MTA looks at the destination address provided in the SMTP protocol (not from the message header), in this case *recipient@rec.org*. An Internet e-mail address is known as a Fully Qualified Domain Address (FQDA). The part before the @ sign is the local part of the address, often the username of the recipient, and the part after the @ sign is the domain name. The MTA looks up this domain name in the Domain Name System (DNS) to find the mail exchange server accepting messages for that domain.
3. The DNS server for the *rec.org* domain, *ns.rec.org*, responds with an a Mail Exchanger (MX) record listing the mail exchange servers for that domain, in this case *mx.rec.org*, a server run by the recipient's ISP.
4. *smtp.send.org* sends the message to *mx.rec.org* using SMTP, which delivers it to the mailbox of the receiver.
5. The recipient presses the 'mail' button in his MUA, which picks up the message using the Post Office Protocol (POP3).

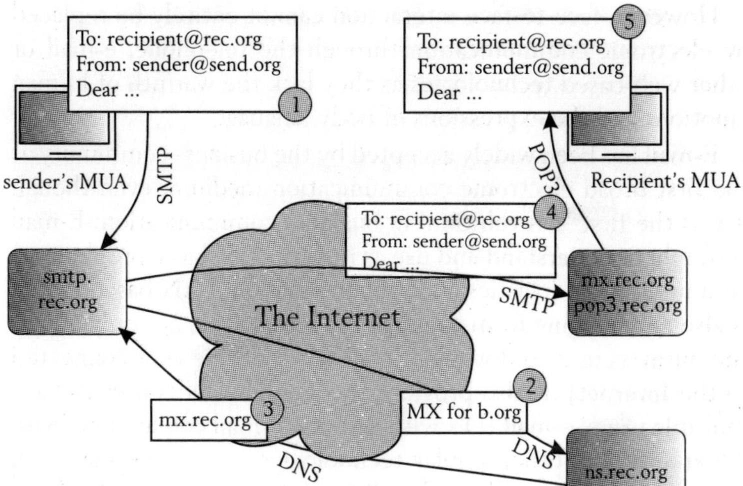

Although this sequence of events applies to the majority of e-mail systems there are many that may function differently.

USES AND ABUSES OF E-MAIL

In most advanced economies, e-mail has become the preferred mode of communication both for social and business purposes. It has, to some extent replaced the face-to-face meetings and communication. Landline telephone systems and mobile telephony are other popular methods of communication today. Face-to-face meetings are no more the primary form of social communication as globalisation, privatisation and liberalisation have made societies and communities more mobile than at any other time in human history.

It is an established fact that in economically advanced countries of the world, people actively use e-mail to maintain core social networks, particularly when they are located at a great distance from those they wish to contact. With an increase in Internet usage, there is a decrease in the use of other modes of communication. Proficiency of Internet and e-mail use serves as a mediating factor in this relationship.

However, face-to-face interaction cannot entirely be replaced by electronic communication through the telephone, e-mail or other web-based technologies as they lack the warmth of human emotions and the expressions of body language.

E-mail has been widely accepted by the business community as the first broad electronic communication medium, even though it was the first 'e-revolution' in business communication. E-mail is simple to understand and use as it solves two basic problems of communication: logistics and synchronisation. LAN based e-mail is also an emerging form of usage for business. It not only allows the business user to download mail when offline (not connected to the Internet), it also provides the small business user to have multiple users' e-mail ID's with just one e-mail connection. With 'bluetooth' and other similar technologies, e-mail messages can be received and sent through cell (mobile) phones which put an executive in touch with his business any where, any time. It can connect several devices, overcoming problems of synchronisation. In fact, most recent laptops come with a built-in bluetooth adapter, which helps in receiving and sending e-mails.

Though a popular form of communication for social and business purposes, e-mail has both advantages and disadvantages.

Advantages

Like any technological device, e-mail has both—uses and abuses. Let us first consider its advantages over other forms of communication in the areas of logistics and synchronisation.

As the business world relies upon communications between people who are not always physically present in the same building, area or even a country, e-mail becomes very handy for establishing communication. Telephone calls or teleconferencing, though give the freedom of oral communication, have their own inconveniences. Besides being expensive, this needs the presence of a caller and a receiver, at a mutually convenient time. This may pose difficulties if the caller and receiver are in multinational locations. E-mail provides a way to exchange information with no set-up costs and is generally far less expensive than physical meetings or phone calls.

Synchronisation is a major problem in making a telephone or conference call. In multinational companies different branches are in different time zones. It is therefore difficult to set up a teleconference that suits the convenience of all the employees. This problem can be taken care of by exchanging e-mails.

Disadvantages

Reading, ordering, sorting, 'recontextualising' fragmented information, and writing e-mails takes a lot of time of employees due to an increasing use of e-mail. It can therefore lead to some of the problems listed below:

- **Loss of Context**: Because most of the e-mail services do not allow all the messages from one source to be stored collectively, these messages are likely to lose the context. Tracking such messages and putting them in folders is a difficult job.
- **Alienation of Individuals**: Nervous or poor speakers in face-to-face situations have started taking recourse to e-mail to communicate, which leads them to become less sociable, and alienated. If this trend of impersonal communication becomes the dominant form of communication, it is feared that people may not invest time and effort in developing conversational skills.
- **Inconsistency**: Due to information overload, e-mails tend to duplicate information. Sorting this overload can lead to inconsistency. If a large team is working on a number of documents that are duplicated, a lot of time will be wasted in sorting the information.

Despite these disadvantages, e-mail has become the most widely used medium of communication in the business world. It is also gaining popularity in social world through 'chat groups' and social networking sites such as 'Orkut', 'Facebook', etc.

Spamming and Computer Viruses

E-mail bombardment, spamming, phising and e-mail worms pose a huge threat to e-mails. Millions of dollars are spent every year on creating softwares to protect e-mail users from such threats.

Spamming is unsolicited commercial e-mail. Because of the very low cost of sending e-mail, spammers can send hundreds of millions of e-mail messages each day at very low cost. Spamming results in information overload as this uncalled for e-mail takes a lot of time to read and discard. Though most e-mail services like Google, Yahoo, Hotmail, etc. have set filters to check spamming, spammers out smart these filters and penetrate the system.

E-mail worms are the viruses that find a way of replicating themselves into vulnerable computers. These worms travel through e-mail and corrupt your computer. They are capable of crashing the system totally. Hence a number of anti-virus systems such as Norton Antivirus, Aviva Antivirus, etc. have to be used to protect them from these attacks. Many countries including US, Canada and Australia have passed laws to take action against those who create virus systems.

Privacy Concerns

Privacy is a major concern with Internet Service Providers (ISPs). Most e-mail messages have to go through intermediate computers before reaching their destination, which makes it easy for others to intercept and read messages. Almost all ISPs store copies of our e-mail messages on their mail servers before they are delivered. They keep their backups for several months on their server, even when they are deleted from our mailboxes and for these reasons some companies do not trust the privacy of e-mail messages.

REFERENCES

Castells, Manuel. 1996. The Information Age: Economy, Society and Culture. Vol. 1 of *The Rise of the Network Society*. Oxford: Blackwell Publishers.

Friedman, Thomas L. 2005. *The World is Flat: A Brief History of the Twenty-first Century*. New York: Farrar, Straus and Giroux.

Guffey, Mary Ellen. 2000. *Business Communication: Process and Product*. Cincinnati: Thomson South-Western.

Chapter 4

Non-verbal Communication

It is wrong to assume that we communicate only when we speak or write. Even when we are not engaged in an oral conversation or in a writing activity, we may be communicating something. That is done through the use of our body. In fact, non-verbal cues speak louder than words. Non-verbal communication refers to all external stimuli other than spoken or written words, including body motion, characteristics of appearance, voice and the use of space and distancing. These include all unwritten and unspoken messages both intentional and unintentional. These silent signals exert a strong influence on the receiver. Generally, when a speaker is transmitting a message of joy, automatically the body responds by way of facial expressions, gestures or the movements of the hand. Same is the case when anger, sorrow or frustration is expressed. In such cases the verbal and non-verbal cues correlate. But at times the verbal and non-verbal messages contradict each other confusing the receiver. In such situations the receiver places more emphasis on the non-verbal cues to decipher the message. Successful communicators recognise the power of non-verbal messages and use them to achieve the greatest impact.

Elements of Non-verbal Communication

The figure given below helps us understand the importance of non-verbal cues in communication.

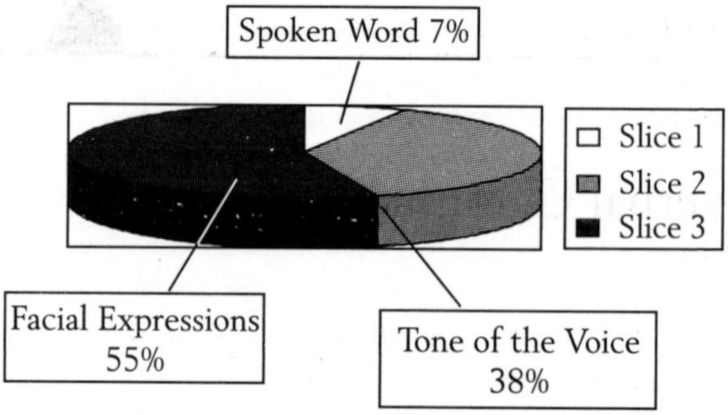

These numbers tell us that facial expressions and the tone of voice that contribute maximum to meaning-making. Let us now look at the different non-verbal cues a communicator uses in order to transmit his/her message.

A. Body Language/Kinesics
1. Appearance
2. Facial expressions
3. Gestures
4. Posture
5. Eye contact

B. Space and Distancing/Proxemics
1. Space
2. Territory
3. Time

C. Modulation of the Voice/Paralanguage
1. Pitch
2. Tone
3. Volume
4. Rhythm
5. Intonation

BODY LANGUAGE/KINESICS

Appearance

The physical appearance of an individual transmits immediate and important verbal messages. The way you look—your clothing, posture and gait transmit personality traits to the audience/receiver. They make quick judgments and form an opinion about your status, credibility, personality and potential even before a single word has been uttered. One's appearance may put the audience in a receptive or a hostile mood. If they are in a receptive mode and your message does not interest them, then you can be rejected. Conversely, if they have formed a negative attitude about you looking at your appearance and your speech and message impresses them, then their attitude will turn positive. Appearance always forms the first impression of a presenter in the minds of the audience. A well dressed, elegant person therefore makes good impression on the audience.

Certain dress codes have been established for formal and informal occasions. Generally at the work place people are formally dressed. However, this may not be the case in the IT sector that has redefined this convention. In some IT companies today, only one day a week is reserved for formal clothing while on other days the employees can dress informally. Certain organisations have a dress code top-down, that is, the entire staff wears a uniform. This is usually done to obliterate hierarchy in an organisation.

Situations dictate the type of clothes one needs to wear. For instance, during interviews, presentations or during formal situations, it is understood that formal clothes need to be worn. Flashy garments, heavy jewellery, garish make up, overpowering fragrance of perfumes and colognes need to be avoided. Apart from clothing, attention should also be paid to grooming. A good haircut, body cleanliness, polished shoes, etc. reflect a well-groomed personality.

Facial Expressions

The expressions on a communicator's face are as revealing as his/her speech. 'Human face can display 2,50,000 different expressions,' says Ray Birdwhistle (1970). Raising or lowering one's eyebrows, squinting the eyes, swallowing nervously, clenching the jaw, smiling broadly and many more voluntary or involuntary expressions supplement or, at times replace entirely the verbal message. A wooden expression on the face of the speaker frustrates the audience while brightness in the eyes keeps the interest and the enthusiasm sustained.

Eye Contact

The eyes are an extension of the mind and the window of the soul. It is said that the eyes accurately reflect the true feelings and emotions of the speaker and the listener. Looking straight into the eyes and saying something signals trust and truthfulness. One's eyes can express focus, receptiveness or distance. Eyes are the biggest feedback marker for a sender. If the eyes of the recipient wear a blank expression, the message has not been received or comprehended. Continuous eye contact with audience helps the speaker/communicator to alter, reframe or adjust his/her message. This process of eye contact between the sender and the receiver is an unconscious act. Studies have shown that better eye contact leads to more effective communication. It is therefore necessary that a conscious effort be made to look at all sections of the audience. If the gaze of the speaker is on the ground, on the ceiling, on the door or on any object other than the audience, however good the speech may be the speaker will fail in communicating the message to the audience. Eye contact, therefore, should span all sections of the audience so that no one feels ignored.

Posture

Posture of an individual silently conveys many traits from self confidence to shyness. Posture refers to the way one stands, walks or sits. A good, confident speaker stands tall, with his/her shoulders upright, keeping the chin at right angles to the spine balancing his weight equally on both the legs. A discouraged, tired and worn-out speaker can be recognised by his/her drooping shoulders and protruding stomach. Similarly, the gait of the speaker also either attracts or distracts the audience. Leaning towards the speaker suggests interest and attraction while pulling away or shrinking back denotes fear, distrust or anxiety.

The way the speaker sits can be indicative of the speaker's success or failure. A speaker sitting on the dais is watched by the audience who form their own opinion of the speaker depending on the way he/she sits, stands or walks. Remember that different situations demand different sitting postures, the ideal being to sit with the back up straight from the waist, both feet being slightly apart but firmly placed on the floor.

The walking posture conveys whether the speaker is confident, energetic, vital, withdrawn, nervous, etc. You should be able to walk across the stage with ease and grace because people watch with interest whether the speaker is shuffling/dragging his feet or taking long or short strides. These body movements have to be consciously cultivated in order to project oneself positively and allow the audience to form a favourable impression of you before the first words are spoken.

Gestures

The importance of gestures as a medium to communicate cannot be undermined. Entire thoughts are conveyed through simple body movements. A well-timed gesture can effectively drive home a point. Playing with a ring, twisting key chains, tapping a foot or making a noise with a pen while you are speaking mar the effectiveness of communication. Even wringing of hands is a sign of nervousness which sends wrong signals to the audience. All talking is accompanied by gestures; in fact it is near impossible that one speaks without the use of any movements of the hands, head or the shoulders. Though these occur unconsciously they certainly contribute a great deal to the message being conveyed. But, we must be aware of the gestures we are making. For instance, the use of too many gestures can create a negative impact on the audience. Looking at oneself in the mirror to practice before a presentation or interview is a good way of ensuring that you do not use unnecessary gestures. Speakers who are not using gestures adequately can consciously include some to drive home certain points. This would definitely help in becoming an effective communicator.

One must also keep in mind that these non-verbal cues are culture specific. And therefore each gesture could be attributed different meanings depending upon the context in which it is used. For instance, a team member who signals a success sign by forming the thumb and forefinger into a circle would be in deep trouble in Germany or parts of South America. This harmless 'O.K.' sign is an obscene gesture in those areas. Similarly, a hug in India between two friends is a sign of love and affection, but, in the western countries it would connote a very different meaning. Therefore, when one speaks, depending upon the constitution of the audience appropriate culture specific gestures should be used so that they can contribute to effective communication.

SPACE AND DISTANCING/PROXEMICS

Time, space and territory form three external elements that convey information in the communication process. People convey meaning the way they structure and organise their time and the way they order space around themselves.

Space

The manner in which we arrange things in the space around us speaks volumes about our personality and objectives. Whether the space is a dorm room, an office or a department cabin, people reveal themselves by the design and the placement of furniture within their allotted space. An executive who seats his/her visitors in a row of chairs in front of his/her table indicates aloofness and desire for separation. Similarly, those who stay indoors without opening doors and windows tend to signal the desire for secrecy. On the contrary, a team leader having a semi-circular arrangement of the chairs conveys a desire to be more open and egalitarian in the exchange of ideas. A manager creating an open office space without any partitions seeks to encourage an unrestricted flow of communication and work among different areas.

Territory

Each one of us has a certain territory around us which we do not allow others to invade. For instance, at home your father may have a separate chair in which he is most comfortable, or in the workplace certain employees may feel that particular tools and implements are exclusively their own. All of us maintain these zones of privacy and we interact with each other within that space. The noted anthropologist Edward T. Hall has categorised four zones in which social interaction takes place. These are presented below in the form of a table.

TABLE 2 Four Space Zones for Social Interaction

Zone	Distance	Users
Intimate	0 – 1 ½ feet	Reserved for members of the family and other loved ones
Personal	1 ½ – 4 feet	For talking with friends privately. The outer limit enables you to keep someone at arms length
Social	4–12 feet	For acquaintances, fellow workers, and strangers. Close enough for eye contact, yet far enough for comfort.
Public	12 feet and over	For use in the class room and for speeches before groups. Non-verbal cues become important as aids to communication.

Source: *Business Communication Process and Product* by Mary Allen Guffy.

From the above table we can see that our family members and intimate friends alone are allowed in the intimate zone. If any one violates these unwritten codes, then we are extremely uncomfortable. In such a case we may become defensive and try to re-establish our space.

These zones also differ culturally. For instance, an American or British may not stand as close to another person while speaking as they do in India.

Time

The way we structure and use time conveys our personality and attitude. If a person gives a visitor an appointment and has a long interactive session then it is sending a clear message of the person's interest in the topic and respect for the visitor. On the other hand, if a person repeatedly arrives late for team meetings it speaks of his/her disinterest in it or that he/she accords low priority to it. These are certain assumptions one makes though punctuality is viewed differently in different cultures and regions.

Voice Modulation/Para Language

Voice modulation also forms a very important aspect of effective communication. In spoken communication we need to keep in the following elements of voice explained below.

Pitch : is the tone of the sound depending on the rate of the vibration of the vocal chords. Its variation ranges from the soprano to the bass level.

Volume : refers to the power of the sound and it rages from very loud to very soft.

Rate : indicates the speed at which we speak words. On an average a person speaks about 150 words per minute.

Tone : is the quality of the voice that an individual possesses. Some voices are labeled pleasant if they are found to be soothing to the ears, but at times voices could be jarring and creaking. The tone of the voice reflects psychological arousal, emotion and mood. It may also carry social information as in a sarcastic, superior or submissive manner of speaking.

Intonation : refers to the rise and fall of voice when an individual is speaking.

It is very important to note that whenever we speak it should not be in a monotone (where the pitch, volume and rate is constant). Such voices are very boring to listen to and indicate lack of enthusiasm, vigour and zeal in the speaker. If the speaker speaks too slowly, the thread of the argument is lost on the audience. It also signals a depressed state of mind. On the other hand, if the pitch of the voice is high, with emphasis on the required words, it indicates enthusiasm and excitement. The tone of the voice can also reveal disbelief, astonishment or a questioning attitude. To be a successful speaker, one has to use all these elements effectively. Recording your own voice and analysing it is an effective way of evaluating your voice modulation. This self analysis will help in developing the correct tone, intonation, pitch and volume required to convey a message effectively to the receiver/audience.

To conclude, non-verbal cues are a very powerful medium of communication. We should be aware of their importance in conveying meaning. In order to harness the power of silent messages a ready reckoner of some cues is presented below.

TABLE 3 Handshakes

Sr. No.	*Type*	*Significance*
1	Equal handshake	Equal in behaviour and attitude
2	Tight grasp	Superiority Complex
3	Limp handshake	Inferiority Complex and Dejection
4	Politician's handshake	Deceptively Subservient Position
5	Informal handshakes	Informal Behaviour and Attitude

Source: *Business Communication* by Asha Kaul.

TABLE 4 Voice Modulations

Sr. No.	*Manner of Portrayal*	*Connotation*
1	Monotonous voice	Boredom
2	Slow speed, low pitch	Depression
3	High pitch	Enthusiasm
4	Ascending tone	Astonishment
5	High pitch, long drawn out speech	Disbelief
6	Abrupt speech	Defensive

Source: *Business Communication* by Asha Kaul.

TABLE 5 Hand Movements

Sr. No.	*Manner of Portrayal*	*Connotation*
1	Hugging self	Uncertainty, lack of confidence
2	Arms folded with thumb pointing upwards	Closed mind, superiority complex
3	Holding hands in front	
	Left atop the right	Artistic bent of mind
	Right atop the left	Logical bent of mind
4	Clasping of hands behind the neck	Aristocratic gesture, used by royalty
5	Hands resting lightly on the neck	Analysing a problem
6	Hands clasping the back of the neck	Danger Signal
7	Scratching the head	Perplexity
8	Stroking of the chin	Ideas being given careful consideration
9	Lightly scratching or rubbing one side of the neck	Insecurity
10	Clenching of Hands	
	Speaker	Does not believe in what he is saying
	Listener	Frustrated and irritated
11	Both hands or one hand on hips	Signals authority
12	Hands down/fists clenched	Gearing for a showdown
13	Arms folded with thumbs pointing upwards	Closed temperament
14	Rubbing of hands	
	Quick rubbing	Excitement / enthusiasm
	Slow rubbing	Preoccupation / deception

	Rubbing as if hands were being washed	Over with the issue
15	Pressing of hands in front of oneself	Pleading
16	Stapling of fingertips with thumb and first two fingers	Extreme confidence bordering on eccentricity

Source: *Business Communication* by Asha Kaul.

Activities

1. What attitudes do the following body movements suggest to you? Do these movements always mean the same thing? What part does context play in your interpretation?
   a. Whistling, wringing hands
   b. Bowed posture, twiddling thumbs
   c. Steepled hands, sprawling sitting position
   d. Running hand through hair
   e. Open hands, unbuttoned coat
2. In groups of five, discuss the kind of silent messages one sends to one's instructors, classmates, and employers in various contexts. Talk about how these messages are sent and what they mean.
3. Match the techniques in Column A with the relevant skills from Column B.

Sr. No.	A	B
1	Establish and maintain eye contact.	Make non-verbal assessments only when you understand a situation or a culture
2	Use posture to show interest.	Appropriate eye contact signals interest, attentiveness, strength and credibility

3	Reduce or eliminate physical barriers.	Keep in mind that the appearance of your business documents your business space and yourself send immediate positive or negative messages to receivers.
4	Improve your decoding skills.	Learn about other cultures to widen your knowledge and tolerance of intercultural nonverbal messages.
5	Probe for more information.	Ask them to monitor your conscious body movements and gestures to help you become a more effective communicator.
6	Avoid assigning non-verbal meanings out of context.	Encourage communication interaction by leaning forward sitting or standing erect and looking alert.
7	Associate with people from diverse cultures.	Move out from behind a desk; shorten lines of communication; arrange meeting chairs in a circle.
8	Appreciate the power of appearance.	Ensure that your verbal and non-verbal messages are in sync by taping and evaluating yourself making a presentation.
9	Observe yourself on video tape.	Watch facial expressions and body language to understand the complete verbal and non verbal message being communicated.
10	Enlist friends and family.	When you perceive non-verbal cues that contradict verbal meanings politely seek additional cues.

REFERENCES

Birdwhistle, Ray. 1970. *Kinesics and Context*. Pennsylvania: University of Pennsylvania Press.

Guffey, Mary Ellen. 2000. *Business Communication: Process and Product*. Cincinnati: Thomson South-Western.

Kaul, Asha. 1998. *Business Communication*. New Delhi: Prentice Hall of India.

Chapter 5

Effective Listening

Most of us do not realise the importance of listening as a communication tool. It is an acknowledged fact that we listen a lot more than we read and write. Since the act of hearing comes naturally to us like the act of breathing, we do not place much emphasis or pay any attention to it because we just 'hear' and not 'listen'. Listening is nothing but hearing with intention. As soon as we listen to or read something, the tendency is to analyse and interpret it and this analysis, interpretation and the action taken after that is foregrounded while the basic act of listening is relegated to the background. One must not undermine the importance of listening. In fact, development of listening skills holds the key to effective communication. The effectiveness of communication depends on a number of factors of which listening and comprehending are the two most important ones. In the course of a full interaction, keen listening skills help in reducing confusion and misunderstanding.

While hearing may be an involuntary and casual activity, listening is a voluntary and serious activity and therefore has to be planned deliberately.

In the entire process of communication, it is estimated that more than 50% of the time is spent in listening, 30% in speaking, 16% in reading and writing takes only the remaining 9% of the total time spent on full acts of communication. The human mind has the capacity to process 400 words per minute while the average speed of a speaker is 125 to 200 words per minute. Because of this gap between the time taken in speaking and the much less time taken in processing this information, the human mind remains unutilised for half the time that the speaker speaks to the listener. During this idle state, the mind is diverted and starts wandering . Hence, during this period of distraction, whatever the listener hears is not understood by him/her. By the time the listener focuses on the speaker again and tries to understand what the speaker is trying to say, he/she realises that a lot of information has been missed out on. Such a lapse in listening results in misunderstanding of ideas, concepts, and descriptions provided by the speaker. Therefore, listening is one of the most important and challenging skills to develop for effective communication. By developing the ability to listen well we also develop the ability to reproduce much more accurately. This refines our understanding and enhances our ability to communicate effectively.

Hearing therefore is the understanding or the perception of the spoken matter from our own point of view while listening is an accurate understanding and perception of all that is being communicated by the speaker. To listen, thus, is to hear accurately.

Sometimes, it also happens that we listen to only those portions of what the speaker is saying that we are interested in. This means that we listen selectively. Though we have heard what the speaker is saying only some of the matter is absorbed.

FACTORS THAT ASSIST LISTENING

Listening is a complex mental activity, an integral part of the communicative process. There are many factors involved in a successful act communication. The mental capabilities of the listener, along with verbal competence, play an important part in fully understanding a message.

The listener must have knowledge of the language and its nuances. Both these factors put together send appropriate signals to the brain that process information and allow the listener to comprehend what the speaker is trying to convey. In addition to this, the motivation and interest of the listener enables him/her to understand the sender's message. If there is a lack of motivation then the listener would also lack alertness of mind to receive the message. There would be lapse in concentration, resulting in information loss that could prove detrimental to the message. Contextualisation is another important factor, particularly when the speaker is unknown and the subject that he is talking about is also unknown. When we listen in our everyday lives we hear language within its natural environment. This familiar environment gives us clues about the linguistic content we are likely to listen to. However, listening to a stranger with an unfamiliar accent about an unknown product or service that you need, has to be a deliberate act as you are taken out of the original environment and context. Hence, for effective listening to take place, there is a need for contextualisation.

Therefore, to aid the listening process it is important to have verbal competence, motivation, and certain amount of intelligence so as to contextualise the message for business purposes.

THE LISTENING PROCESS

An important intent of listening is for accurate reproduction. This can happen only when there is a full understanding of the meaning that the speaker is trying to convey. This is a complex process that involves the following three levels or phases:

1. Levelling/Sensing/Receiving
2. Sharpening/Attending
3. Assimilation/Understanding

Let us try to simplify this complex process. Just as a farmer prepares his land to sow seeds, the human mind is similarly kept open to receive any information at all the three above-mentioned levels. All types of sounds heard are received by the mind. They are then processed through a 'mental filter'. This helps the mind to sift the sounds that have been heard. The filter then sifts the 'sensical data' from the 'non-sensical data'. The sensical data is stored in our minds as mental representations having a meaning while the non-sensical data is discarded or kept away for future use. This stage is called 'sharpening' or 'attending'. These new mental representations are mapped on to the old ones that are already present because of continuous experience and exposure to the outside world. Where the mind of the individual perceives a discrepancy in the meaning between the new and the old mental representation, the listener asks questions, seeks clarifications and tries to understand what the speaker is trying to say. When he/she understands the meaning and responds appropriately, we can say that assimilation has taken place and the message has been assimilated and understanding is complete according to what the speaker intended to convey. Thus, it may be noted that the communication was effective.

To summarise, at the first level of the listening process, only sounds are heard and no understanding takes place. Then with the help of knowledge, past experiences and intelligence, evaluation of the sounds heard takes place and understanding begins. Lastly, the listener requires empathy, skill, and concentration to understand the speaker's message fully.

TYPES OF LISTENING

When we ask the audience to reproduce what they just heard in a presentation, we receive different versions of the same speech. This happens because each member of the audience listens differently. Each individual hears the message from his/her point of view and contextualises it within their own experiences and perceptions to arrive at an interpretation of the matter presented. This happens because of the type of listening done by an individual. Some listeners are passive, others are marginal and still others are active listeners. This brings us to the section on the different types of listening.

There are five types of listening as discussed below.

1. Passive
2. Marginal
3. Projective
4. Sensitive/Empathetic
5. Active

Passive Listening

This type of listening means that the listener is physically present but mentally absent. In this type, though the listener hears all that is said, he does not understand its meaning fully and hence assimilation does not take place. Much of what is heard turns into verbal garbage and is thrown out of the mind. In such cases, the listener fails to follow the line of thought of the speaker and misses much of the information and the important points. This type of listening is common in classroom situations and the teacher has to devise different strategies to bring back the mental faculties of the students to what he/she is explaining. It is also likely that this type of listening may take place during a presentation, if the audience is not motivated or if the speaker does not offer any new points. It may also happen when speaker speaks in a monotone or rattles off too much information without creating any visual impact. In such situations, listeners are likely to switch off their mental faculties and even go to sleep.

Marginal Listening

If too much of information is inflicted upon the listener, it may go waste resulting in marginal listening. This creates superficial understanding, as the listener is not interested in understanding the subject fully. This kind of listening may also cause boredom and fatigue. Marginal listening leads to miscommunication or bad communication, which is not good for business.

Projective Listening

Each individual has a point of view on a particular topic. This point of view comes in between the sender and the receiver. While listening to the speaker, the receiver tries to understand the topic from his point of view and not as the sender intends. This results in the listener understanding the message from a narrow perspective, which causes misunderstanding and miscommunication.

Sensitive Listening

In this type of listening, the receiver tries to understand the intended message of the sender. As noted earlier, a message does not mean the same thing to everyone. Each one tries to understand it from his/her perspective. However, there are receivers who try to match their perceptions with that of the sender. In order to understand the senders' point of view the receiver raises questions and seeks clarifications where the message is unclear. The response of the sender enables the receiver to understand the message as the sender intended it. This also means that the strategy of empathising is used. Empathy means to put oneself in someone else's place to understand another's feelings. By empathising with the sender, the receiver is in communication with the sender and is making an effort to understand the message that is being conveyed.

Active Listening

This is the most important type of listening. Active listening is a structured form of listening. In this type, the attention is focused on the speaker. The listener must take care to attend to the speaker fully, and then repeat in the listeners own words, what he/she thinks the speaker has said. It is not necessary that the listener has to agree with the speaker. He/she must simply state what the speaker has said. This enables the speaker to find out whether the listener has really understood him/her well. If the listener has not, the speaker can explain once again what he intended to communicate. The listener can also raise queries and seek elaborations and explanations on words, ideas and issues so that the message can be completely understood as the sender intended it. This means that communication is effective only when there is participatory contribution from the receiver. Active listening has several benefits.

- Firstly, it forces people to listen attentively to others.
- Secondly, it avoids misunderstandings, as people have to confirm that they have really understood what the speaker has said.

- Thirdly, it tends to help people open up and say more. When people are in conflict, they often contradict each other. This tends to make people defensive. At this stage, they either lash out, or withdraw and say nothing more. However, if they feel that their opponent is really attuned to their concerns and wants to listen, they are likely to explain in detail what they feel and why. If both parties in conflict do this, the chances of being able to develop a solution to their problem become much greater.

Summary

To summarise one can say that more than half of oral communication is misunderstood because of faulty listening skills. Listening accurately and effectively is difficult because people vary in their communication skills and clarity of expression, as we have often seen that people have different needs, agendas, and purposes for interacting with each other. This indicates that we need to know how to do more than just hear what people say; we need to listen actively to what they are saying. Active listening involves effort, as it is more than focusing on facts, figures, and ideas. Active listeners absorb what they hear, associate it with their own experiences, and convert what they retain as meaningful information that they can use in future.

Objectivity is a crucial element in effective listening. If you lack objectivity, the meaning of the message is distorted and you may jeopardise your relationship with the person communicating the message. React sensibly and fairly to what is being said. Concentrate on hearing the message before you react. Objective listening requires one to seek the total meaning of a message—and not to be hung up on every detail. If you do not understand something completely, ask for clarification so that you are well aware of the meaning of the message.

Here are some tips that you can use to become an active listener.

- Maintain eye contact with the speaker.

- Lean forward and listen with your whole body, not just with your ears.
- Pay attention to the other person's body language, facial expression and tone of voice; these are all a part of the message.
- Nod to show your agreement with particular points.
- Do not let yourself be distracted by unimportant noises or interruptions.
- Put aside any items (pen, paperclips, etc.) you might be tempted to fiddle with.

Activities

1. Most of us believe that we are good listeners. It can be very helpful to get an insight into how others perceive our listening skills. Ask your colleague, spouse, a close friend, your child or a trusted co-worker for a few minutes of their time requesting them to be absolutely honest. Ask the following questions, and be prepared for some new insights into your own behaviour.
    - Am I a good listener?
    - Are there times when I 'tune out'? When does this happen?
    - What would make me a better listener?
2. Certain situations are given below. Identify what type of listening is involved.
    a. 'A' wants to convey an important message to 'B'. 'B' is unable to understand completely. He asks questions and asks 'A' to elaborate on certain aspects of the message.
    b. Suresh's teacher is explaining the theory of communication to the class. Suresh gets distracted as he sees his friend Ram talking to a group of girls outside the class. After his friend goes away, Suresh reverts back to the explanation. He realises that the teacher has already completed the main point and has started explaining the sub-points of the theory.

c. Rakesh has had a sleepless night due to a problem at home. He is in class but unable to concentrate or understand anything.
d. Rahul Bharadwaj conveys a policy decision to his co-workers. Of them, Ritesh Shah interprets the decision in his own way, thereby completely misinterpreting the management's point of view.
e. The Head of the Department in a meeting is apprising the members of the details of a project awarded by the UGC. The faculty members verified the details by asking questions, seeking clarifications, and elaborations on certain points in order to understand the scope of the project and the role they would have to play in it. They also contributed by way of suggestions for the smooth implementation and execution of the project.

3. Record a 30-minute segment of TV news. Listen to it and make a list of the following.
   - Major news items
   - Places, names and figures

   A day later, listen to the same news item. This time do the following.
   - Make selective notes
   - Paraphrase major issues
   - Interpret the figures

Chapter 6

Making Presentations

Making presentations, is an act of oral communication that for some is a cakewalk but for many a nerve-wracking experience. It is not easy to take centre stage and hold the attention of an audience. Nevertheless, it is possible to overcome this fear and make effective presentations. Before we discuss in detail how presentations need to be made, let us first discuss the main objectives of making a presentation.

Aims/Objectives

The word presentation suggests giving information on a particular topic or the act of making something publicly available, like presenting news or other information by broadcasting or printing it. In the context that we are concerned with, presentation is the process of disseminating information or knowledge to a group of people or an audience that either has basic or no knowledge of this topic. The presenter does not go guns blazing to convince the audience of his/her point of view. In fact, he/she tries to present the information logically in a structured manner. It is likely that the audience may get convinced or may not accept the speaker's point of view during a presentation. The purpose of making presentations may be summarised as follows.

- To demonstrate a service, a product or a system
- To entertain colleagues, friends or an unknown audience
- To sell a concept, product or idea
- To represent a group, company or department
- To promote an attitude or work culture

- To suggest a solution or a new concept
- To motivate an audience to a desired activity or goal

Whatever may be the reason for making a presentation, the basic objective, however, is that of communication: that is, transference of meaning from the presenter to audience.

Following are the important points to keep in mind to give an effective presentation.

1. Time
2. Audience
3. Content
4. Audio-visual aids
5. Language

TIME

While making presentations the most important aspect to keep in mind is the 'time factor'. Firstly, we should know how much time has been allotted for the presentation and secondly, what time of the day the presentation is to be made. These two factors help the presenter understand the mood of the audience. Of the two, the former is the most important and the presenter must remember not to exceed the time allotted to him/her. Not only does the audience start fidgeting and getting bored after the allotted time is over (unless the presentation is exceptionally important or interesting), but also, the presenter feels insulted when the audience starts booing, passes uncomplimentary remarks or walks out of the hall. It is the audience's method of showing displeasure or dissent. It is analogous to the situation when a teacher over shoots her/his allotted time limit for a class. It is usually seen that the concentration level of the audience is at its highest in the early stages of the presentation in anticipation of what the speaker is going to say and at its lowest at the final stages when the presentation is nearing the end of the allotted time. Therefore, it is best to tap the audience at its optimum level of concentration. The following diagram will help speakers to structure their presentation according to the time allotted to them.

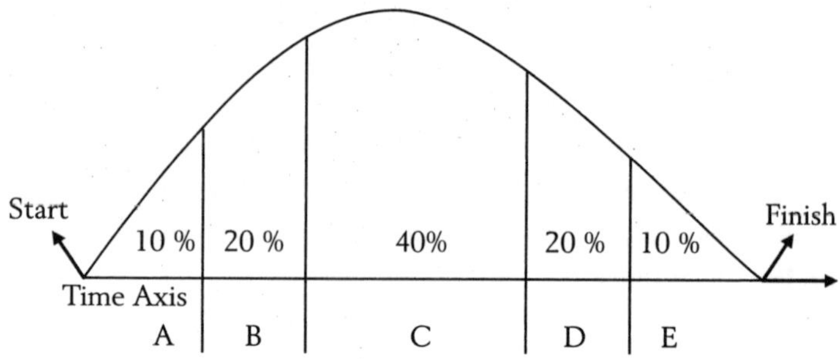

FIGURE 16 Structuring a Presentation

The first 10% of the time allotted (A) should be spent in introducing the topic and developing rapport with the audience. You need to start on a pleasant note with the help of a catchy, witty, and attention grabbing sentence or a hypothetical illustration. A popular proverb or a humorous anecdote may draw attention of the audience easily towards you. If this has an element of surprise in it, it gives rise to curiosity in the mind of the audience as to what the speaker is going to say next. This helps in motivating the audience to listen. In the next 20% of the time (B), you should place a general outline of the topic you are speaking on. After that you may introduce the main points you wish to present. The next 40% of the time (C), the largest chunk of time, should be allotted to explaining the points in detail logically and rationally. This should be substantiated with the help of examples, visuals, audio clips, film clips, anecdotes or any other interesting details that would drive the point home. Visuals such as photographs, transparencies, power point slides, film clips, etc. used at this stage help in making the presentation more effective as an image always has a greater impact on the minds of the audience. We will discuss visual aids in detail in the next chapter. Depending on the actual situation, the next 10% of the time (D) should be spent in explaining the application of what has been presented. This also means that the audience needs to know how the theory presented can be applicable to their daily work requirements or their day-to-day activities. It should be noted that no new points should be introduced at this stage because the audience's concentration is on the wane and it is least receptive at this stage. In the final 10% of the time (E), the speaker needs to summarise all the points and draw the speech to its logical close. The final minute or seconds could be used to thank the audience for their patient hearing.

This is with regard to how you need to manage the given time, but the content you are going to present is of utmost importance. In the next section, let us see what you need to keep in mind while developing the content of your speech.

Developing Content and Preparing the Speech

Before you actually start collecting materials on what to say, it is important to know the profile of the audience you are going to address. Answers to some basic questions given below will prove beneficial in focusing on the content of your speech.

- What is the background of the audience in terms of age, intelligence, education level? Is it homogeneous or diverse?
- How knowledgeable are they in the topic you wish to present?
- Would your ideas be acceptable to them?

Once you answer these questions, you are ready to begin the process of preparing the content of the speech in the following four stages.

1. Collecting materials/information
2. Sifting through materials
3. Writing the speech
4. Timing, practicing and rehearsing

Collecting Materials/Information

In the first stage, all available information has to be collected on the topic you wish to speak on. You could begin your search for material with the Internet by using a reliable search engine like Google. A search through online newspapers like *Times of*

India, Hindustan Times, Indian Express, The Hindu and many others with their own search tools would be very useful for contemporary subjects and topics. Wikipedia, though not reliable for a presentation on a scholarly topic, is another source for a quick reference.

A visit to a good library for collecting material from books, magazines, periodicals, archives, and online journals would be helpful. For interviews of eminent people in the field, observations and comments on their work, visits to specialised libraries and institutions would be beneficial. Designing questionnaires for feedback may also be useful.

SIFTING INFORMATION

Once this has been done, the next step is to read all the materials and gradually arrive at a perspective on the topic you wish to speak on. This would enable you to sift the collected material. The materials you feel would help you to focus on the topic should be picked up for immediate use, while the remaining material should be kept aside for future use. Your reading should now focus on the point of view you wish to develop and present.

WRITING THE SPEECH

Once the ideas become concrete, it is time to write out the speech. Write down all the ideas that come to your mind without editing. This is known as 'free writing'. Each point in your presentation needs to be placed logically in the order of importance and then explained lucidly and explanations should be substantiated with the help of examples. These examples could be from the workplace if you are addressing an audience that has some similar work experience or from everyday situations so that the audience can understand it. It is advisable not to use hypothetical examples as the audience may not relate to it and thus misunderstand your message. The draft has to be written and rewritten several times until you are fully satisfied and confident that your presentation contains all the points you want to include in a manner in which the audience will be able to understand it. Once you are satisfied with the written draft of your presentation, it is time for editing. Look for points that sound repetitive, unnecessary or irrelevant and remove them. Fine tune sentences and correct any errors in grammar or vocabulary. After the final draft is ready, you may place the visuals you wish to show at the appropriate places, taking care that there is no mismatch between the explanation and the visual. In order to avoid any confusion it is better to write the title of the visual below the text it follows so that as soon as you finish explaining the text you remember that you have to show that slide or transparency.

TIMING AND REHEARSING

After the final draft is ready, it is important to practise and 'time' your speech. As mentioned earlier, speaking only during the allotted time is very important. Keep a stopwatch by your side and read your speech aloud to find out the exact time you would be speaking for. If what you have written overshoots the allotted time then you have to delete some portion of your speech. While doing so you are likely to be in a dilemma about which portion of the speech to delete. You definitely need to retain the main argument. However, if in order to explain the argument you have added many examples, it is better to retain only the example that best explains the point and delete the others. By doing so you will not only save on time but also succeed in putting across only the most relevent points to the audience. You also need to keep in mind that you have to show the visuals within that time frame. It is likely that showing all the visuals could be time consuming, therefore, like the examples sift through the visuals you wish to present and select only those that highlight your point of view and make the presentation interesting and challenging. Other visuals could be shown to the audience later or perhaps during the question answer session when the context arises. Once you are absolutely sure that your speech would not exceed the given time limit, it is important to rehearse it in front of a mirror. This would give you an idea about the gestures, mannerisms, intonation patterns, and rhythm of your performance. Perhaps you could improve on that if you feel that you are doing too many of them. For improving on your speech, and language, you may record it on a tape recorder so that you listen to it carefully and improve upon it. Video recording of your performance could also be very helpful, particularly if you can get the opinion of a friend or appreciative critic. However, do not get the opinion of an unsympathetic critic at this stage, as it may dishearten you.

On the day of the presentation, be calm, cool, collect your thoughts, check the equipment you will need to use and wait patiently for your turn to come. When it comes make a powerful presentation putting your heart and soul in it.

TYPES OF AUDIENCES

As explained above, the content of the presentation depends on the type of audience you are going to present to. One cannot exactly know the complete profile of the audience. Nevertheless, some preliminary information about the audience needs to be obtained (this has been dealt with in the previous section). Even then, one cannot predict the reaction of the audience accurately and therefore, it is essential that while presenting one needs to be aware the type of audience that is likely to be present. Let us analyse some of the main types of audiences and discuss their characteristics.

Superiors

Many a time presentations will have to be made to one's superiors. No doubt, it is a daunting task, but if one is well prepared and knows the subject that he/she has to speak on thoroughly, it would go a long way to lessen the initial nervousness. Therefore, to ensure that the presentation is successful one must organise the data carefully and concisely. If you are questioned on something that you are not adequately informed about then be honest and admit it. Most importantly, have a positive attitude to criticism. In addition, you need to be assertive but not to the point of being arrogant or aggressive.

Colleagues

It is a very challenging and dicey task to make a presentation in front of your colleagues especially if there is rivalry. They may resent or object to the ideas or changes that you propose. In such situations, you have to present your views in a firm and a convincing manner without being aggressive because ultimately you have to work with them for its implementation. You should also accept their suggestions and respond positively to their queries.

Team

Presenting as a team leader is different from speaking to your team mates on a day-to-day basis. The members of your team would expect a lot of preparation, knowledge, and confidence from your side as you are their leader. If you present your ideas in an informal way you will be commended on your friendliness and sincerity which in turn would go a long way in getting your ideas across to them. Finally, you must be open to incorporating the suggestions of your team members if they are practical and contribute to the outcome.

Mixed Audience

When you are addressing a mixed audience, you are unsure about the type of response or feedback you are likely to receive from them. The reason is that you are unaware of their level of knowledge on the subject. It is best to begin by assuming that they have the basic knowledge on the topic you are presenting. The language used should be simple as far as possible. It is better to avoid jargon and technical words to enable the entire audience to understand what you are saying. The materials therefore, should be presented from different angles and perspectives so that a sense of common purpose can be created.

Hostile Audience

You may face an audience that is resistant, biased or unsupportive. The best way to face such a group is to be thoroughly prepared with your subject and to use the time to the maximum, taking care not to exceed the allotted time. You must analyse the audience well so that you can be prepared to answer any questions or queries they may put to you. Try to stay calm and do not get argumentative. Counter negative reactions, politely but firmly. Build on points of agreement.

International Audience

Robert Moran, Philip Harris and William Stripp (1989) note that if we are addressing an international audience it is very important to consider the cultural differences, that exist between different nations and communities. Analysing responses of people from different cultures, he notes their differences as follows:

- Japanese audience: look for sincerity. They go deep into the inner meaning of what the speaker has said.
- French audience: are interested in statements that are fully supported with facts and figures.
- American audience: favour the practical aspects. They like to explore how things work in a practical way.
- German audience: tend to focus on the technical aspects; therefore, the speaker must be technically sound.
- Swedish audience: are likely to pose more theoretical questions and expect the speaker to define strategies.

It is important to keep in mind that no section of the audience is hurt on account of the points presented or the examples given to further explanation.

Presentation Techniques

It is not enough to write a good speech with a good introduction, body and an apt conclusion. It is equally important to present it in front of the audience in a proper manner. You should therefore keep the following aspects in your mind while making the presentation.

1. Language
2. Appearance
3. Voice
4. Body language

5. Notes
6. Visual aids
7. Answers to questions

We shall deal with the use of language and notes as well as answering questions in this chapter; the remaining aspects are discussed in other chapters of this book.

Language

Using appropriate language forms a very important component of any presentation. Not only does the language have to be grammatically correct, but also the choice of words must be appropriate. The words used should not be ambiguous, as double meanings confuse the listener. Use of jargon (specialised technical terminology characteristic of a particular subject) should be avoided, particularly if you are addressing a non-technical audience. When the audience encounters too many words that they don't understand, they get distracted and lose concentration. So, as far as possible, words used in everyday life should be used so that the audience is in a position to understand what the speaker is trying to convey. The use of transitions in speech is also very important. In writing, we write about one idea in a paragraph and start a new paragraph when we are discussing another idea or subject, thus marking a transition. We also use linkers and transitional markers for the smooth flow of the text, helping the reader understand the message better. Similarly, while speaking, to emphasise the transition from one idea to the other, verbal transitions like *firstly, secondly, finally,* etc., should be used. Some transitional phrases like *in addition to, besides this, looking ahead, in spite of this, to conclude, in contrast to,* or words like *however, nevertheless, consequently, later, next,* etc. not only add to the flow of your speech but also make the presentation a coherent whole. Even non-verbal transitions in the form of body movement or silence can be used. For example, a pause of a few seconds between the introduction and the body of the speech can be an extremely effective transition marker.

Asking questions is also a very useful and effective strategy. When a question is thrown to the audience, it immediately starts thinking and formulating an answer to the question. Further, when the speaker presents his/her opinion it acts as a confirmation to their thinking. If their thinking matches with that of the speaker, they understand the speaker's point of view; when there is a disparity it may result in a question being asked in the question-answer session. This strategy also helps in drawing the attention of the audience to what the speaker is presenting.

In order to make the audience easily understand what you are saying, ensure that you use short precise sentences in your presentation. Long winding sentences need a longer span of attention. Use of long and convoluted sentences will blur the main idea that the speaker is trying to convey. The meaning is lost on the audience and misunderstanding and misinterpretation is likely to take place.

One should also avoid the use of slang and colloquialisms (informal language consisting of words and expressions that are not considered appropriate for formal occasions) as they are open to misinterpretation. As the audience is not listening to unravel verbal puzzles, the language used should be clear, concise, appropriate, intelligible and easy to understand. In addition, you should speak in an enthusiastic, interesting and a motivating manner with passion that should fire the imagination of the audience.

Using Notes

It is useful to keep note cards in front of you while making a presentation. An outline of the presentation can be written on these note cards. In legible handwriting, write only the main points and sub-points. Ensure that the points are written in correct sequence. It is advisable to number the cards so that even if they fall down or are scattered, the sequence of points is not lost. You may also use different coloured ink pens, so that you know exactly which point to highlight while speaking. Even a change in the tone and pitch or a pause and gesture can be indicated with the colour of the ink. Look at the sample note card given below. You can see that only the heading, main points and sub-points are written on the card. The double spacing between two points that is, point A and B acts as a punctuation marker and denotes that the speaker has to pause for some time before explaining the second point. Preparing note cards in this manner helps the presenter logically sequence her/his presentation, creating an impact on the audience.

Elements of Non-verbal Communication

A. Body Language/Kinesies

1. Appearance
    a. ____________
    b. ____________
2. Facial Expressions
    a. ____________
    b. ____________

B. Space and Distancing/Proxemics

1. Space
    a. ____________
    b. ____________
2. Territory

01

FIGURE 17 Sample Note Card

Answering Questions

This is one of the most important segments of a presentation. It is certainly a challenging proposition to answer the questions raised by the audience. The first thing you must do is to listen very carefully to the question asked. Answer the questions in a straightforward manner and take care not to be rude to the questioner even if the answer to the question was already covered in the presentation. Instead, you should understand that the question is asked despite your explanation. This only means that you need to elaborate on the point some more in order to make it clearer. Illustrate your point at this juncture with more examples so that the questioner is in a position to understand your point better. It would also help if the point is explained all over again. You could also show the visuals again and use some other examples to clarify the doubts. This would also help those listeners who have doubts but lack of confidence to ask questions. When members of the audience put forward opinions contrary to your own, acknowledge them graciously and explain your stand on the issue without getting defensive.

CONCLUSION

When you are asked to make a presentation follow the tips given in this chapter and you will find yourself a more confident speaker. One must remember that it is experience that makes one learn. We are bound to make mistakes. However, these mistakes should become our learning strengths and stepping stones. Each presentation you make will help you overcome nervousness, build confidence to face the audience better.

Activities

1. The toughest part of preparing an oral presentation is forming and developing an outline. Select a topic and prepare an outline for your presentation using the following format and guidelines.

   Title

   Purpose

   I. Introduction

   - Gain attention of audience
   - Involve audience
   - Establish credibility/rapport
   - Preview main points
   - Transition

   II. Body

   - Main point
   - Illustrate
   - Clarify/contrast

Transition

- Main point
- Illustrate
- Clarify/contrast

Transition

- Main point
- Illustrate
- Clarify/contrast

III. Conclusion

- Summarise main points
- Provide final focus
- Encourage questions

2. Enumerate, analyse, and discuss effective techniques for adapting your oral presentation to a cross-cultural audience.
3. Why is it necessary to repeat key points in a presentation?

REFERENCES

Moran, Robert T., Philip K. Harris and William G. Stripp. 1989. *Developing the Global Organization: Strategies for Human Resource Professionals*. Houston: Gulf Publishing Company.

Chapter 7

Audio-visual Aids

Audio-visual aids include audio or video recordings, paintings, pictures, cartoons, graphics, charts, film clips, newspaper clippings, etc. These help make a presentation effective and help the audience relate to and retain the presentation. Any presentation that is made without such aids is incomplete and may not be as effective. However, an excessive use of these materials may divert the attention of the audience from your presentation. They are used not only for embellishment and ornamentation but, have a definite role to perform. Any presentation is easier to understand and remember when suitable graphics are presented. They form an essential part of any presentation as they help in communicating your message effectively.

Purpose

One must remember that audio-visual aids are not a substitute for verbal presentation. They clarify and supplement verbal analysis, description and discussion. If chunks of spoken material are presented the audience starts getting bored. Instead, if certain written materials are placed before the audience in a visual form, the session becomes more interesting, lively and the message gets transmitted more effectively.

Visuals help present large amounts of data succinctly and with greater precision. Often an integrated picture needs to be presented in which there is a comparison of different items, their analyses and interpretation. At such times explanation becomes a cumbersome process both for the speaker as well as the audience. If visuals are used at such times, explanation becomes easy for the speaker while understanding the message becomes an interesting experience for the audience. At times, complex data involving numericals need to be presented. The same information may be summarised in a table, a chart, or a graph. This means that effective graphics:

- clarify meaning
- simplify complex ideas
- clarify data
- condense and simplify data
- emphasise data

There is also an aesthetic aspect to it. Most people find colourful, illustrated material more lively, interesting and intellectually appealing than blocks of written material in black and white. Illustrations capture the reader's attention quickly and transmit the message effectively. But this does not mean that all types of visuals can be used for any presentation. The area/topic of the presentation lends itself to the use of certain types of visuals. For example, if one has to compare and contrast numerical data on the marketing of the same Fast Moving Consumers Goods (FMCG) products produced by the rival business houses, then displaying pictures and maps will not suit the objectives. Instead, depiction of data through graphs and charts would be more appropriate as this helps the speaker compare and contrast data. The audicence would also find it easier to understand the marketing strategies of rival business houses. This means that visuals need to be selected according to the topic and data you wish to highlight.

TYPES OF AUDIO-VISUALS

With technology, newer mediums of presentation have come about. There are two types of audio visual presentations—the traditional and the technologically-generated ones. Given below is a summary of the traditional visuals in use and their objectives.

TABLE 7 Traditional Visuals and their Objectives

Visual	Objective
Table	To show exact figures and values
Bar Chart	To compare one item with another
Line Chart	To demonstrate quantitative changes over a period of time
Pie Chart	To visualise a whole unit and the proportions of its components
Flow Chart	To display a process or a procedure
Organisation Chart	To define a hierarchy of elements
Photograph/Map/ Illustration	To create authenticity/to highlight a location/ to show an item in use

Source: *Business Communication: Process and Product* by Mary Ellen Guffy

Technologically generated visuals which are currently used in the corporate world are discussed below.

Overhead Transparencies

Transparencies are a common aid used by students and professional speakers. Most auditoriums are equipped with screens and projectors and hence the speaker is only required to prepare the transparencies according to the requirement of the presentation. Acetate transparencies for the overhead projector are cheap, easily available and can be prepared either by hand, on a computer or by a copier. When you prepare transparencies by hand or on a computer the following points should be kept in mind.

- Use a special overhead projector (OHP) marker to write
- All information should not be condensed into one transparency
- Use separate transparencies for separate ideas
- Information should be presented in point form

- Font size should be large enough for the audience to read

A little elaboration on how and what to write on a transparency will help at this stage. As mentioned earlier it is better to write only points on a transparency. As far as possible avoid writing long paragraphs as the audience may not be in a position to read everything. At the most definitions of a concept may be written so that the audience can grasp the entire meaning. The size of the letters should be large enough for people sitting at the back to be able to read it without straining their eyes. Different colours can be used to write different points and ideas in order to capture the attention of the audience. You can also mask some information in an already prepared transparency until the relevant point is reached.

The major advantage of using transparencies is that you can continue to maintain eye contact with the audience. Care should be taken to stand on one side of the projector so that you do not obstruct the view of the audience. Transparencies are a simple technological aid that can be used to make a presentation more effective.

Computer Visuals

Now-a-days professionals and public speakers have switched to computer presentations and visuals as it is more economical, flexible and easy to prepare. One can create dynamic, colourful visuals on the PC using different softwares like Microsoft Powerpoint, Freelance Graphics, Corel Presentations, etc. These programs are generally shown on a PC monitor, TV screen, LCD panel or a screen. These visuals can be supplemented with stereo sounds, videos and hyperlinks to create an impact and attract the attention of the audience.

Power Point

The professionally designed templates that come with a software program called Microsoft Powerpoint are the most commenly used to make presentations. This software offers numerous options to choose from. You can select a layout page for the title, a bulleted list, a bar chart, a double column list, an organisation chart, etc. according to the subject of the presentation. You can make a slide colourful by choosing a colour scheme. Background and text colours can be selected keeping in mind the lighting in the room where the presentation is going to be made. Generally, light colours are used for text on a dark background in a darkened room while dark text on a light background is used in lighted rooms. This should be kept in mind even while making transparencies. Same colour should be used for like elements, for example, all slide titles should be of the same colour and sub-titles of another colour.

While preparing and using slides some points need to be kept in mind. The main topics of the presentation forms the titles of the slides. The sub-points may be presented as bulleted items. These items should not be full sentences, only phrases or key words; like in the example given below.

Purpose of the Study

- To determine awareness of campus recycling program
- To recommend ways to increase campus awareness

FIGURE 18 Sample Slide

In an electronic presentation there are in-built ways and means of drawing the viewers attention to the point you are presenting. The bulleted items may 'fly' from one end of the screen to the other, horizontally or vertically, the point may appear on the screen letter by letter, etc. In preparing a bulleted list you can use the 'slide transition' component to provide effects like 'wipe out', 'glitter', 'ripple', etc. Be careful not to go overboard with these effects. It is better to apply only one effect to all the slides. That is, if you have chosen the 'ripple' effect for the first slide then it is better that to apply the same effect in all subsequent slides. The reason for this is that, on seeing the first slide, the viewer's mind gets accustomed to accept certain kind of visual effect. In the next slide if there is a change in the effect and the position of the matter, it is likely that the viewer's mind may take a little time adjust to the visual change. In the time that is lost to get accustomed to the change perhaps the viewer may lose the thread of the argument which the speaker is trying to make. This may result in misunderstanding of what the speaker is trying to convey. This becomes a major disadvantage to the speaker because despite adding visuals to the presentation, their meaning may be lost on the viewers defeating the basic purpose of the visuals.

While writing the text on the slides, the 'rule of seven' needs to be adhered to. That is, each slide should include not more that seven words in a line and not more than seven lines should be written on a slide. Presentation slides only summarise the information the speaker wishes to convey; they do not tell the whole story.

In order to enhance the content you may also add multimedia effects like, sound, animation and video elements. These capture the attention of the audience. Photographs can also be presented as low cost scanners and digital cameras are easily available these days. Thus, technology provides numerous opportunities to the speaker to tap its potential and use it judiciously to communicate effectively.

Speaker's Notes and Handouts

Electronic presentations offer numerous options. They can be complemented by distributing pictures, outlines, brochures, articles, charts, summaries or even miniature versions of the slides. The timing and distribution of the handout is integral to its effectiveness. If you distribute the handouts in the beginning then, the content of the presentation is exposed, thus making the audience lose interest while you are speaking. If the handouts are distributed while you are speaking, again they will get distracted and they will lose the thread of the argument. Perhaps the best time to distribute these supplementary materials is after the entire presentation is over. There are a couple of advantages in this. Firstly, it acts as a reinforcement of what you have said.

Secondly, the audience can carry it home with them, read it at leisure and understand your point of view better. There is another advantage which is more psychological. The audience feels that you have given them something useful which can be preserved for later use.

But this is not a norm. If the speaker wants the audience to know something before hand, as a reference point then the speaker can give the handout at the beginning of the presentation. This would help the audience to contextualise and understand what the speaker is trying to say. For example, if the speaker is talking about certain architectural descriptions, it would help to give out pictures of the structures before it is spoken about.

The following table details the advantages and disadvantages of various mediums of presentation.

TABLE 7 Presentation Enhancers

Sr. No.	Medium	Audience Size	Formality Level	Advantages & Disadvantages
1.	Overhead Projector	2–200	Formal or Informal	Transparencies are easy and inexpensive to produce. Speaker keeps contact with audience.
2.	Flipchart	2–200	Informal	Speaker can prepare the display in advance or on the spot. Easels and charts are not readily available and difficult to transport.
3.	Write-and-wipe board	2–200	Informal	Porcelain on steel surface replaces the messy chalk board. Speaker can wipe clean with cloth or duster. Requires physical effort.
4.	Slide Projector	2–500	Formal	Slides provide excellent graphic images. Darkened room may put audience to sleep. Slides demand expertise, time and equipment to produce.

5.	Video Monitor	2–100	Formal or Informal	A VCR display features motion and sound. Videos require skill, time and equipment to prepare.
6.	Computer Slides	2–200	Formal or Informal	Computers generate slides, transparencies or multi-media visuals. Presentation softwares are easy to use, and produce the best results.
7.	Handouts	Unlimited	Formal or Informal	Audience appreciates take-home items such as, outlines, tables, charts, reports, brochures, summaries. Handouts can divert attention from speaker.

Look at the following table for tips on preparing and using slides. Happy presenting.

Table 8 Tips for Preparing and Using Slides

- Keep all visuals simple
- Use the same font size and style for similar headings
- Apply the 'rule of seven'
- Make sure that everyone in the audience can see the slides
- Show a slide, allow the audience to read, then paraphrase; do not read from the slide
- Rehearse by practicing talking to audience, not to the slides
- Bring back up transparencies/slide prints in case of equipment failure

Activities

I. Identify the most appropriate audio-visual aid to illustrate the following data. Illustrate the data using the graphic representation of your choice.

1. The academic, administrative and operation divisions of a university
2. A comparision of the sales of VCRs, colour TVs and PCs over the last 10 years
3. Areas in India where earthquakes occur
4. Percentages of students opting for different professional disciplines

II. Tabulate the following data in terms of characteristics, area, population, economy and ethnic groups.

<u>Sumatra</u>

It is the largest island in Indonesia. *Area*: 481,780 sq. km (the size of California). *Population*: 38 million. *Economy*: Based on oil, natural gas, rubber, palm oil and tobacco. *Ethnic groups*: over 15, including the strongly Muslim Acehnese, the extroverted Bataks and the matriarchal Minangkabau.

<u>Bali</u>

It is the best known island in Indonesia with over a million visitors annually. It is called the 'Island of the Gods' for its many deities and Bal-Hindu religious festivals. *Area*: 5,532 sq. km., the size of Hawai. *Population*: 2.6 million, *Economy*: Wet-rice agriculture and tourism. *Ethnic groups*: Balinese

Java

It includes the capital city of Jakarta with 9 million inhabitants, the nation's political, administrative and economic center. Area: 130,398 sq. km. (the size of England). Population: 115 million, Economy: Wet-rice agriculture and manufacturing. Ethnic groups: Sudanese, Madurese and Javanese.

Kalimantan

It is the Indonesian portion of Borneo. Area: 549,032 sq. km. Population: 9 million. Economy: Based on oil, natural gas, and trading in the coastal cities; subsistence agriculture in the interior. Ethnic groups: Malays, Chinese and Bugis in the coastal cities, numerous Dayak groups in the interior.

III. Why are visual aids particularly useful for inexperienced learners?

IV. Why are transparencies a favourite visual aid?

V. Explain the advantages of electronic visuals.

REFERENCE

Guffey, Mary Ellen. 2000. *Business Communication: Process and Product*. Cincinnati: Thomson South-Western.

Chapter 8

Interview Techniques

A job interview is a kind of marketing for gainful employment. In an interview, candidates get the opportunity to prove their professional skills and justify their qualifications, abilities and experiences. The applicants also get a chance to understand the strategies and prospects of the prospective employer as well as to explain their curriculum vitae and to sell their professional skills. In addition, an interview is also an occasion for companies to promote themselves and explicate the duties and responsibilities of the job they are hiring for.

Often job interviews are the cause of tension and stress in a lot of candidates. At the same time, there are those who look forward to receiving interview calls and enjoy the prospect of exploring the market for better job opportunities. Those who do not like to be evaluated or judged are afraid of rejection. It is possible to overcome the feelings of fright and anxiety before the interview by keeping a few tips in mind and preparing carefully. Guidelines in this chapter are intended to help an interviewee feel free, confident and comfortable at an interview.

There are some questions, which may be asked in one form or other in an interview. It is a good idea to reflect on the kind of answers one may give but it is not advisable to memorise answers. This may result in nervousness and fumbling if you is not able to reproduce the answer as memorised. It will also result in anxiety when unexpected questions are asked. Therefore, one has to be prepared to face an interview where run-of-the-mill questions are not asked. It is a good idea to back up your answers with examples taken from your own experiences.

It is very important to impress the interviewer by paying full attention to what is said and taking interest in the proceedings of the interview. You should always look attentive—so do not droop in your chair. Never lie during an interview as your body language and tone of voice may give you away. Classic body language giveaways include scratching your head, playing with your fingers or holding the handle of the chair or side of the table and not looking straight at the other persons, when you are speaking to them. All these body cues will reveal that you are uneasy and uncomfortable.

Interview Problems

The following are some of the questions you must ask yourself before an interview.

- Do you lack confidence for that all-important job interview?
- Can you handle difficult questions and devise convincing answers?
- Are you out of practice in handling interviews?
- If an interviewer uncovers any of your weaknesses, do you know how to handle it?
- Do you have any specific problems that you are particularly worried about such as being over/under age, or over/under qualified?
- Do you have the problem of making a career move upwards/downwards, changing career, trying for a job after redundancy/unemployment/pregnancy/sickness, etc.?
- Are you anxious about your interview performance?
- Are you worried how you would be able to beat your rivals and secure the job that you want?

Given below are points to keep in mind before an interview.

1. **Be prepared**: Know the company. Research its history, products, and reputation in the market. A quick search on the Internet may

help you in this. Try to know what kind of person the company is looking for this job.

2. **Try it on yourself**: Think through your answers before you arrive for the interview. It is a good idea to try answering the questions in front of a mirror.

3. **Know yourself**: Be prepared for a brief presentation on the highlights of your career. Prepare answers to likely questions. Bring extra copies of your resume. There may be several people on the panel.

4. **Show interest**: Be enthusiastic. People love to select individuals excited about their company. Present a positive attitude. Remember companies seek pleasant and amiable employees. Humility is always appreciated. Do not make the interviewer guess that you want the job badly, even if you do so.

5. **Sell yourself**: As the interviewer does not know the real you, it is up to you to effectively convey a sense of who you are. Take pride in your expertise and experience as well as other skills and talents, and tell the employers how they will benefit the company.

6. **Look good**: The first impression is very important. Make a strong first impression by taking time to establish eye contact, smile, and firmly shake hands with each person on the panel. If you are introduced to a group of people, you shake hands with each with an impressive smile. Above all, be pleasant and look confident.

7. **Cooperate:** If the interviewer is new to the company, offer encouragement. If the interviewer is a veteran of the company, let him enjoy his break from the typical daily grind. Let him talk if he seems to enjoy it.

8. **Dress code**: It is better to be over-dressed than under-dressed. Your appearance will demonstrate that you are taking the initiative. Even if you never wear a suit to work, the interviewer will be pleased by your effort to impress. If you are a male, never go for an interview wearing sandals/chappals, a T-shirt or an untucked

shirt as these give the impression of being casual and not serious about the job. See that your shoes are formal and polished as informal and unpolished shoes display lethargy and tardiness.

9. **Be early**: You cannot recover from being late, so play it safe and reach early. Remember that it takes time to sign in and to complete other official formalities and paperwork. Make sure that you know exactly where you have to be for the interview. If you are not familiar or not sure of the place, make a trip to the company/office the day before the interview.

10. **Be attentive**: Interviewers rely a lot on body language to determine your level of interest. Sit straight, make eye contact, and avoid crossing your arms or legs. Listen carefully to what the interviewer says. Make sure you express that what they are saying is of importance and of interest to you.

11. **Be honest**: Do not hesitate to state your weak and strong points clearly and honestly. If you do not know the answer to a question asked, admit it. Your honesty will be appreciated.

12. **Be calm and composed**: Most people get nervous during a job interview. Sit quietly for a few minutes before the interview and clear your mind by taking deep breaths. When you need it, take a moment to think before answering or asking a question. If it is not for very long, the interviewer can only interpret this as thoughtfulness—and that is a good thing.

13. **Practise:** Practise your interview with a friend or a well-wisher to defuse the fear of the interview. Informal chat is the best way to start. Here is an easy way to start: find something in the office (or the lobby) that is interesting and comment on it to lighten up the atmosphere.

14. **Do not overreact**: No matter what happens, do not overreact to matters such as salary, location, or other issues. It is always possible to negotiate these issues later when you are selected for the job. However, this does not mean that you should not put forward your views on these issues. When asked about these issues, make your demands clear and inquire about the facilities and perks that go with the job.

- Are you competitive?
- What problems did you encounter in your last job and how did you overcome them?
- Do you feel you are ready to take on greater responsibilities?
- What are you like under pressure? What are your strategies for handling pressure?
- How many hours are you prepared to work?
- What are your career goals?
- How did you get on with your last manager/colleagues?

All interviewees have certain apprehensions, questions and queries in their mind. Given below are some such questions and the answers to them.

How should I dress?

Dress to feel confident and to show respect. Wear clothes that you think you would wear to an important meeting on the job at that company. Do not under dress.

What should I bring with me?

Bring copies of your resume, original testimonials and certificates with a sufficient number of copies in a folder that can be opened conveniently. In this folder keep also a writing pad and a pen that writes well. The pad might be handy for taking notes. The pen shows that you are adequately prepared to face the interview.

How much should I research the company?

You should research it enough to describe the following: their main products, their performance in the past few years, their main competitors, and trends in their industry. You should also have an idea about how you can help the company to rise above its competitors.

Where can I find information on companies?

If you are a college student, there is often a good deal of recruitment information available at your placement office. Otherwise, you can use the Internet. The organisation's website is the best place to start with. Good summaries are often found in the 'About' section of these websites. Sections for investors often include annual reports, which give you enough information about the company. Reading professional journals, trade magazines and periodicals would be an additional advantage for you. Some of these journals/magazines/periodicals may be freely available on the Internet.

What is the best way to talk about yourself during an interview?

Always keep the following in mind while talking about yourself: a. talk about your accomplishments, and not about your duties and b. turn each statement about your past into a statement about how it would help you to do a good job if you have to work for the company and position you are being interviewed for.

What is the best way to improve the way I carry myself in an interview?

Role playing is an effective way of preparing for an interview. Make a deal with friends: they pretend to be interviewers for you and you pretend to be an interviewer for them. Ideally, you should also role-play with someone who is willing to give you candid criticism.

If during an interview I get a job offer of my choice, should I immediately accept it?

It is not advisable to accept the job immediately. Give yourself some time. Ask for a few days to consider it. Ideally talk awhile about the whole package—salary, equity, bonus, benefits, housing and relocation. It shows maturity and interest. It also prepares you for negotiations that may be necessary before you accept the job offer.

How can I reduce my anxiety about the interview?

Here are the two time-tested ways to reduce anxiety about the interview: a. know more about the company than the interviewer knows about you and b. role-play using difficult questions and do not forget to relax before the interview through deep breathing

way meeting. The interviewer is evaluating you, but you are also evaluating that company to determine whether you would like to associate with it as an employee. Pay attention to the following when you have to face a team of interviewers.

- Be sure to connect your responses with each person at the interview.
- Have eye contact with the person asking questions and glance at the other team members while answering the question.
- Be sensitive to the dynamics in the team. If they seem to want to control the interview, relax and comply with it, on the other hand be sure to offer information and ask questions.
- Take responsibility to ensure that the group understands what you have to offer. The best approach is to be sensitive and adapt your approach to the group. Do not be excessively aggressive and take over, yet do interact and show your enthusiasm.
- Each person's opinion can be weighed equally; in some cases, just one team member's opposition can disqualify a candidate. Sometimes it is unclear what role or position a person in the team holds; therefore, you need to be respectful of everyone at the interview.

YOUR QUESTIONS

Try to think of some questions to ask at the interview. If you have researched the company well, you will be able to come up with questions concerning the organisation. You may also want to find out more about your responsibilities and your role, the organisation's long and short term aims, training opportunities, overall organisational structure and what they would hope you achieve within the stipulated period.

Some questions you could ask

- What do you think makes the company more special than others in the similar field?

- How would you describe the culture in the company?
- What are the typical traits of the company's successful employees?
- What are the job classifications in the career ladder in the company?
- What is the typical career path for someone like you?
- What are the long-range objectives of the company?
- What does the company excel at?
- What are the areas the company is working to improve?
- What outside influences can affect the growth of the company?

Other things to remember

Do not look at your watch: The interviewer's time is at least as important as yours. The interviewer has other candidates to interview as well. Let the interviewer be the timekeeper, so you can focus on your performance and get involved in the interview, if you are really interested in the job. Looking at your watch will mean that you are impatient in the job and hence the employer may not take keen interest in you.

Tentative answers: Avoid giving tentative answers. Do not say things like: I'll try . . . I'll do my best . . . I hope . . . possibly . . . if it's really necessary . . . I suppose I could do that . . . I've never done that before, but . . ., etc.

Follow the interviewer's lead: Throughout the dialogue, the interviewer would give you additional information and lead your focus on particular aspects of the discussion. Respond adeptly, even though you might feel that some other aspects are more important.

Appreciation: After the interview, you may write a letter or send an e-mail thanking the interviewer/s for the time they spared for you and the opportunity they gave you to express yourself and the experience you gained. Indicate your appreciation of their friendly treatment and the excellent hospitality you received.

Chapter 9

Group Discussion

People often get together to talk on a particular topic. The topic is discussed, the pros and cons analysed, and then a conclusion is arrived at. This type of talking is generally called a discussion. However, when we use the term 'group discussion', we do not mean a causal conversation. The term implies a planned meeting that has a specific purpose to achieve. The following definition perhaps will make the concept clearer. A group discussion is the oral exchange of ideas between three or more people, usually under the direction of a leader for the purpose of enlightenment, solving a common problem or satisfying a felt need. When we analyse the definition, we can identify the following salient features of group discussions.

- It is an oral exchange of ideas
- Three or more people are involved
- It is conducted under the direction of a leader
- Such a meeting has a specific purpose

Thus, a group discussion with all the above-mentioned features is a form of oral communication like an interview or a presentation, in which exchange of ideas, information, thoughts, and opinions take place. Unlike a presentation where only one person presents his/her opinion at a time, in an allotted time period, or in interviews when only one person can be interviewed at a time for any given post, in a group discussion, a minimum of three people must be present to discuss a given topic. There could be more than three participants but there is also an outer limit to the number of people that can take part in a discussion, which is discussed later in this chapter. Apart from the participants forming the core, there is also a leader who guides the entire discussion giving it a particular direction. The role of the leader/moderator is also discussed separately. Finally, a discussion does not take place just because people have met. There is a purpose attached to any discussion taking place and the purpose of holding a group discussion is elaborated below.

PURPOSE/S OF DISCUSSION

As mentioned earlier, a group discussion is not a casual conversation; it has a definite goal or purpose.

1. The most important purpose of holding a group discussion is to determine the action to be taken regarding a problem according to the need of the group. For example, the department of English of a university wishes to hold an inter-faculty poetry reading competition. To hold such a competition, a meeting of the department would be called to discuss the following points.
   - Benefits of such a competition
   - Details of the competition
   - Ways of implementing the competition
   - Finding ways to fund the competition

   In other words, the reason or the purpose for holding the discussion would be to initiate action towards fulfilling the need of the group.
2. Another reason to hold a discussion is to formulate a policy or establish attitudes. For example, a department has bought some computers and a meeting is called to discuss the formulation of policy for its use. Such discussion might be followed by direct action. From this example, we understand that a discussion was held in order to form a policy, which would be implemented by the members. Current events and issues are good discussion topics. Discussions on these are likely to be followed by direct action in the form of signing petitions, voting and legislation.
3. A discussion could be held just for an exchange of information. For example, certain topics in the syllabi of the courses offered by the English department lend themselves

would not matter much but definitely to include members from post graduate classes or those who are working would not be advisable as it would change the level of discussion and put the first year students to a disadvantage. Similarly, if the discussing group comprises members from various industries then at least six to seven members out of nine should possess approximately the same number of years of work experience. Care should be taken not to have a group whose members' age level and work experience are very different form each other, for example, where the work experience of the participants in a discussion ranges from 1 to 20 years. This varied exposure could lead to such situations where numerous differences would surface and the group may not be able to reach a decision. Therefore, similar status of the participants results in more friendliness, more interaction and fewer restraints on the group members.

Discussion Format: The formality or the informality of the discussion, the presence or the absence of the observers, the method of selecting the leader and the degree of freedom that the participants possess, all these factors will have an effect on the group. Although an authoritarian approach may prove useful in problem solving, in the long run, democratic procedures prove to be more useful and beneficial. All the members should get equal opportunity to voice their opinions, to enter the discussion and to come out of it, to assert to either support or oppose what the other members are saying. This means that parliamentarian procedures should be followed in group discussions. This places a lot of responsibility on the moderator to ensure that the discussion progresses in the right direction and a decision is reached.

Group Norms

Norms are codes of behavior that regulate interaction among group members. Members who disregard the norms will be subtly and indirectly told in various ways to change their behaviour and habits. For example, if a member is habitually late to discussions, he/she could at first be told by the members to be punctual. If the member is still tardy, then the leader or the moderator could impress upon him/her to stick to the time told. If the tardiness persists then the moderator could begin the discussion without that member, or to take one-step further, the moderator could ask another member to join the group.

Cohesiveness

The qualities of group unity and team spirit are the most desirable traits that a group should possess. It improves the morale of the participants and leads to a greater degree of task accomplishment. This trait of cohesiveness is usually associated with the group that meets often or perhaps at regular intervals. Also homogeneous groups in terms of age, educational background, work level, etc. would probably develop more cohesiveness than a heterogeneous group comprising dissimilar individuals. A clearly defined purpose and a sense of commitment to a cause also make a group cohesive.

Task Commitment

How quickly the group completes the given task depends upon the immediacy and importance of the problem discussed and rewards involved thereafter. Rewards may be peer approval, self-satisfaction, and material benefits. This results in higher motivation for the participants. It is analogous to a classroom situation in which the students are motivated to do better and give their best if they are to get good grades as their reward; even the praise of the instructor is likely to strengthen a student's efforts.

Forces affecting Individual Members

While constituting a group, one may keep in mind the various physical characteristics mentioned above, but ultimately the discussion that takes place is an example of individual behavioural characteristics. These behavioural attitudes cannot be overlooked. These need to be recognised because they can prove useful or be detrimental in a discussion being successful.

The first of such an attitude is the **desire to control**. Every one has a desire to control others. Some participants reveal this innate trait while the discussion is in progress. The moderator needs to recognise this and channelise the discussion in such a way that it becomes a constructive force and not a disruptive one. For example, if the moderator sees such a dominant trait in one of the members then he/she could assign certain responsibilities to that person in order to implement the task goals.

The **need to belong** or to be a part of the group is also a strong drive in individuals that one needs to address. How strong the urge is to be a part of the group would depend upon the rating that the group has or the prestige that it enjoys. It also depends on what the group has to offer to the participant. For example, a participant may want to be a part of group 'X' because of the choice of the topics that it discusses, or be a part of group 'Y' because of he/she is able to relate to the other participants of the group better. It is also likely that if an individual is assigned a group he/she may not want to be included in it; on the other hand, those individuals who select their own group do it with full knowledge of the consequences. In all the above cases, the satisfaction of being included helps individuals to establish their identities.

Desire for affection is also an attitude which every member wants to fulfill after his/her inclusion in the group. If any team member is not happy with the inclusion of an individual, then it is likely to affect team spirit, the cohesiveness of the team and in turn the discussion process. While the discussion is in progress, the inner conflict is likely to surface creating a dent in the procedure thus, leading to a solution not being achieved.

While discussing, members of the group perform more than one function. In other words, participants adopt roles according to the need of the group. For example, a participant could be a discussant, at the same time an observer and a points recorder or even a devil's advocate. The manner in which she/he fulfills the role and the efforts put in it to achieve it determines the status of the participant in that group. Therefore, it is very important for all participants to have knowledge of the behavioural patterns of the members of the group so that they are prepared to handle these patterns when they surface during the discussion and participants are able to adopt and adjust to these behaviours so that the purpose of the group discussion is achieved.

SELECTING AND FRAMING THE TOPIC QUESTION

In our everyday life we are faced with numerous problems and situations, some urgent, on which immediate discussion is needed and some, on which a discussion though needed, can wait. Therefore, it is necessary to be selective in the choice of the topic. The following points should be kept in mind while selecting a topic.

1. The topic should represent an immediate problem to the group, to the class, to the society or to the nation.
2. The topic is such that it is likely to throw up a satisfactory solution. For example, avoid issues like 'The probability of life after death', because no substantiated material primary or secondary is available, nor can one get first hand information on it. Therefore, a discussion on such topics can only lead to guesses or value judgments and has only 'gossip value'.
3. Choose a topic on which plenty of information is freely available.
4. Topic should be such that the participants are capable of discussing. For example, if a group of non-technical students were given a topic on which technical knowledge is required, then the discussion is likely to to be unsuccessful because of lack of sufficient knowledge of the subject.
5. The topic should be such that meets the needs and interests of the audience. If the discussion is going to be public, it should also be suitable for the occasion.

This clearly means that the topic should be based on practical criteria. Once the topic is selected, the next task is to narrow the focus so that it meets the time limit of the discussion and it includes the important aspects of the topic that the group wants to consider and discuss. An example would make this clearer. Let us try to narrow down the topic 'Juvenile Delinquency'.

First we might narrow it down geographically to incorporate only a particular area or place. We may further narrow the focus by specifically discussing a group based on age, sex, and other factors. Finally, the topic might be limited to certain aspect of delinquency like preventing it, re-educating or punishing the delinquents, etc.

After finalising the topic, the subject of the discussion should be appropriately worded. It is important to phrase the subject as a single question that throws up multiple solutions. It should be free from ambiguity, question-begging words and should allow dissent. Let us elaborate on each of the above points.

The subject should ideally be worded as a question because a question motivates the mind more than a statement. Questions encourage the search for an answer while a statement may suggest a bias. The following example will show you the difference between a question and a statement.

- Statement: Capital punishment should be awarded to all rapists.
- Question: Should all rapists be awarded capital punishment?

You will observe that as soon as a question is asked opinions for and against the topic start framing in your mind. Those opinions that have gained firm roots in your mind ultimately become your point of view which you can substantiate with the help of facts, figures and examples.

After the framing of the topic it is placed before the discussants by the moderator and the discussion begins. The discussion undergoes four stages which are discussed below.

PHASES/STAGES OF INTERACTION IN GROUP DISCUSSION

Aubrey Fisher (1970), states that during a discussion a group goes through four distinct phases.

1. **Orientation Phase:** This is the very first phase and members are more concerned with being acquainted with one another.

They themselves are quite unsure of their own opinion about the topic, hence they are cautious and do not want to open up. They tend to agree to anything that is said, even debatable comments. This tendency to over agree is seen as a strategy to find support for their opinions within the group, so that their points can be presented in a stronger way.

2. **Conflict Phase:** In this second phase, members are more assertive, and positive. They are sure of what they are saying, either for or against the point of view. The expressions are precise, less vague and each point is supported with examples or anecdotes in order to prove it. This is the phase of controversy, argument and dispute.
3. **Emergence Phase:** In this phase, the conflict gradually diminishes. It so happens that if a particular point is seen emerging then the other participants who do not much approve of it realise that they are unable to make a headway and are unable to convince others of their point of view. Such participants, in this phase gradually start withdrawing. Comments and proposals are interpreted more frequently and members do not defend themselves as strongly as they did in the conflict phase. Disagreement is expressed more vaguely.
4. **Reinforcement Phase:** The group's preferred decision becomes more visible during this phase. Argument is no longer important; disagreement seems to vanish; favorable attitudes prevail and there is spirit of general unity.

Role of the Moderator

All discussions have a moderator who sees that the discussion is conducted in an amicable manner and brought to its logical close. What then are the responsibilities of the moderator or the chairperson?

The moderator is responsible for controlling the discussion, clarifying objectives, handling people's opinions, ensuring that all members get equitable time to speak and present their opinions in a frank and a free manner. The moderator should keep in mind not to involve herself/himself with the content of the task however strong his/her opinions are on the topic under discussion. The responsibilities of the moderator are classified into three stages—pre-discussion, discussion and post discussion.

Pre-discussion Stage: Whatever be the purpose or the reason of discussion the moderator needs to make positive moves so that the climate is amicable for discussion. The members should be kept informed about the purpose of discussion. If necessary, he/she also decides on the members needed for discussion. The time and venue of the discussion has to be set and communicated to the members. If some material on the topic needs to be distributed among the participants, it is the duty of the moderator to see that each member receives such material on time. The moderator should let the right tone of formality/informality prevail that is required for the type of group and the discussion that is going to take place. In short, members should be put at ease so that they are relaxed and the best can be drawn out of them.

It is important to begin the discussion on time so that the time of the participants is not wasted. The moderator should greet the fellow group members as they arrive. They should be made to sit comfortably in a face to face seating arrangement. Writing materials, name cards and any other materials required should be provided. The moderator should sit with the group members while opening the discussion. It is better to maintain an informal manner and attitude throughout the discussion.

Discussion Stage: To begin the discussion, the moderator should present the introduction and the objectives of the discussion extemporaneously and in an informal conversational style. However, the topic of the discussion needs to be presented formally after wording it carefully (as suggested in the earlier section). To begin the discussion the chairperson/moderator should start by first asking for the group's indulgence. Further, actual discussion could begin by directing a general question on the topic to the members so that it can act as a catalyst to thinking. The members can then pick up the clue and start placing their opinions on record. If you are the modertor of a discussion in progress, the following points need to be kept in mind.

- Be tactful and objective in your approach. If you dictate to the group, they may take offence.
- Keep ready some questions at hand, so that you can stimulate their thinking. Use these questions only when necessary, that is, when the members become quiet and the discussion has to progress further.
- Keep to the time schedule so that all the points are covered otherwise it is likely that the members may be bogged down by one point which would not leave time for the other points to be discussed.
- Clarify the points that the members make. Even the points, which are in disagreement to the topic, need to be clarified, elaborated and noted.
- The moderator has to oversee that all the members voice their opinion. The shy members have to be encouraged and the members who always 'turn take' and do not leave the 'floor' have to be tactfully reigned in. It is very important to keep in your mind not to take any advantage of the position as a moderator by voicing your opinion, or carrying forward a particular point.
- All points made by the members need to be recorded either on paper or on a black/white board.
- Summaries of the group's progress should be made. This is usually done after each point is discussed and voted on.
- Diffuse any tensions that may result in the discussion not reaching a satisfactory conclusion.
- Finally, sum up the result of the discussion. If necessary, arrange to set up another discussion, time and venue with the help of the group members.

Post-discussion stage: The moderator should immediately prepare a summary of the accomplishments and failures of the group. He/she should make and send copies to all the participants and the agency concerned if it has helped in setting up this discussion.

Finally, she/he must take necessary steps to implement the proposed action agreed upon by the group.

DISCUSSION STRATEGIES

For the success of a group discussion, the members who form the group need to keep a few points in their mind. The most important among these points is that they should state their opinion in clear, concise and precise words. Their sentences should be short and to the point. The other members tend to get bored if a member resorts to a monologue and their attention is diverted. It is also better to state only one or two points at a time so that the members do not get confused.

If you are not very well informed about the topic of the discussion, it is better not to be the first speaker. Yes, it is important to be an even contributor with the rest of the members, but it is more important to crystallise your thinking first. Only when your are absolutely sure, present your views to the group. This would create a lasting impression on the people who are monitoring the discussion.

While your delivery should be crisp in terms of language and vocabulary as stated above, your voice should also play an important role in its delivery. Do not speak very fast. Remember that the other members of the group have to get acquainted with your speech—the formulations of the words, pronunciation, accent, etc. Speaking too slowly may bore the listeners. Therefore, along with a clear diction you need to keep in mind 'talking strategies' so as to create a positive impact on the minds of others.

Finally, keep in mind the cooperative principles of H. P. Grice—Quantity, Quality, Relevance and Manner (discussed in Chapter 1). Once you have the 'floor', make maximum use of it. Do not waste your time indulging in uncommunicative acts because there will be others who are always ready to grab the 'floor'. Also, while making your points adhere to the principles of politeness using markers like 'excuse me', 'please', 'I wish to make a point', etc. because if you are aggressive while voicing your opinion it may not be very well received by the other group members.

To sum up, in this section we discussed how discussions are held in a practical and democratic manner. Some strategies have been suggested so that members can arrive at a consensus decision. Yet, all discussions are not always successful. Sometimes discussions fail due to the faults of the participants, or the moderator or both. Group discussion is an art which one has to master by taking part in it as often as the opportunity presents itself. It is a skill that one has to develop though practice. Only theoretical knowledge is not going to help; hand on experience is necessary to learn it. The first few times it may be difficult to overcome the initial nervousness or present one's opinion in a logical order or in a clear and a precise manner. Nevertheless, with every experience, one is bound to improve and a time will come when this form of oral communication will help you to develop leadership qualities, analytical skills, clarity of thought and the ability to appreciate various points of view.

Activities

I The teacher may divide the class into groups of five students each, appoint a moderator for each group, and assist these groups in selecting and wording a topic. An opportunity could be given to the students to hold preliminary discussion in order to sort out all details before the main discussion.

A few topics for discussion are suggested below.

1. Marriage, career and the modern women
2. Brain drain: A Myth
3. Divorce
4. Right to Information
5. Global Warming
6. Alcoholism
7. Drug Addiction
8. Crime
9. War
10. Commercialisation of Education

a. Narrow the topic down by wording it appropriately so that it can be discussed for an hour and a half.

b. Following the format given below prepare an outline on each of the topics to be discussed

1. Introduction
2. Statement of question for discussion
3. Definition of terms in question
4. List of objectives of the discussion
5. Motivating question to begin the discussion

II Conduct group discussions using one of the topics given below in groups of four or five. Discuss a topic for 10 minutes and then prepare a draft outline of the major points discussed and the decision that the group has reached. The team leader should report the discussion.

- Should an employee be allowed to send personal e-mail messages during breaks or lunch hours? How about using company computers after office hours to do personal work? What would you do if your supervisor gives you permission but asks you to keep quiet about it?
- Should companies have the right to monitor e-mail messages sent by the employees? If so, is it necessary for an organisation to inform the employees of its policy?

Teachers may use the template below to evaluate the students

Discussion Evaluation Form

Name:____

Date:____

Discussion Question:

____

Participants: (The leader should be listed in the first blank and the participants in the remaining blanks in clockwise order from the leader.)

1.____________________ 2.____________________

3.____________________ 4.____________________

5. ____________________ 6. ____________________

7. ____________________ 8. ____________________

9. ____________________

Evaluation of participants: Grade each participant, including the leader on each item below. (1-poor; 2-fair. 3-average, 4-good, and 5-excellent)

	Participant number 1	2	3	4	5	6	7	8	9
1. Knowledge of subject									
2. Analysis of question									
3. Use of evidence and reasoning									
4. Degree of participation									
5. Cooperative attitude									
6. Effective speech									

Evaluation of the Leader

	Grades (1 – 5)
1. Preliminary remarks (introduction)	
2. Guidance of participants	
3. Courtesy and tact	
4. Use of internal summaries	
5. Effective speech	
6. Final summary and conclusion	

Comments and recommendations: (Include organisation of objectives, use of documented proof, brainstorming techniques, preparation of participants, group effort, group rapport, selection and wording of question, open-mindedness and willingness to compromise)

____

____

Source: Speak, Listen, Communicate! by Merritt B. Jones

References

Fisher, B. Aubrey. 1970. Decision Emergence: Decision Making. *Speech Monographs* 37:53–60.

Jones, Merritt B. 1978. *Speak, Listen, Communicate!* New York: D. Van Nostrand Company.

Chapter 10

Preparing an Effective CV

Definition

Curriculum Vitae, is a summary of a person's academic and professional history. CV is the abbreviation of the Latin word 'curriculum vitae', meaning, the course of one's life. Therefore, in preparing your CV, you are essentially describing the academic and professional course of your life to a prospective employer who wishes to use your education, skills and experience to advance her/his business. It is therefore necessary that your CV sells you to a prospective employer. To do this you have to compete against other applicants. The challenge in CV writing is to make your CV more appealing and attractive than the CVs of others who are competing with you for the same job.

To meet this challenge, your CV must be presented professionally, clearly, and in a way that showcases you as an ideal candidate for the job. It should reflect that you possess the right education, skills, experience, behaviour, attitude and morality that the employer is seeking. Effective presentation of your CV demonstrates your ability to communicate and explain a professional business proposition.

How to write a CV

Before beginning to write your CV, put yourself in the shoes of the prospective employer by writing down a description of the person the employer is looking for. To do this, first look at the job advertisement carefully and note down the academic qualifications, skills and experience that the employer wants. Pay special attention to job requirements. Closely examine your educational, curricular and extra-curricular activities, and achievements. Make a list of the projects that you have handled independently or as a member of a team. Now match this information with the listed requirements and prepare a blueprint of your CV. The better the match the more likely you are to be called for an interview.

If you find it difficult to match your own CV description to the job requirements, then perhaps you do not fit the job. Therefore, there is no point in distorting your CV to fit the job. If you falsify in your CV, you will not be able to provide the necessary proof of your claims at the interview. A failed interview is more frustrating than no interview. Lying about your qualifications is a risky strategy, as it can be discovered easily. You should avoid any such temptation. Discovery of a lie leads to loss of reputation, which damages career building permanently. A CV with a lie may cause an embarrassment, or even lead to loss of job when you are at the pinnacle of your glory.

A CV should present you in a positive light. This can be done by highlighting your achievements and capabilities. Writing powerful statements about yourself, it is believed, makes you a strong and positive achiever. Powerful descriptions about yourself, your personality and your strengths and capabilities, in fact, help you become what you wish to be.

TYPES OF CVs

Depending on the job profile, there can be many types of CVs written in different styles. We discuss below two of the more prevalent styles.

1. Chronological

In this type you write the history of your career in a chronological (by date) order beginning with the most recent items in the reverse chronological order. As this is the most popular and conventional approach, it is the easiest to prepare. This type of CV provides a detailed, comprehensive and biographical sketch of the candidate, it therefore works well for 'traditional' students, who wish to present a good all-round mixture of education and work experience. However, experienced people do not like this because it emphasises such factors as age, career breaks and work experience that may not suit the job applied for. Given below is a commonly used format in which CVs are written.

Curriculum Vitae

Name

Address and other contact details
(Phone, e-mail, fax, etc.)

Objective

Experience
1. Employment details
(Dates of employment, name of company, location)

Designation

Job responsibility and achievement

2. Employment details
(Dates of employment, name of company, location)

3. Education

(Date of attendance, name of school, location)

Course studied/degree obtained

Academic achievements

References

2. Skills-based CV

This CV relates your skills and abilities to a specific job or career by highlighting the skills and achievements that matter most to the job that you have applied for. The factual, chronological details of your education and work history are subordinate in this kind of CV, which focuses on the skills and achievements that match the job profile. These work well for high achievers whose education and work experience are not directly relevant to their application.

Some universities and institutions of higher learning have put up material on the Internet to help students make proper job applications. Some of these websites have ready-made templates. Looking at these will help you write your CV effectively. However, use these formats with care as they are designed for specific purposes.

Targetting your CV

If your CV is to be sent to an individual employer who has requested applications in a particular format, you must follow that strictly. But before making the application, research the organisation and the position carefully. This can be done first by searching the Internet and then physically visiting the office, if possible.

Even if you are sending your CV to an unknown employer, it is still important to target it, at the very least, on the general career area in which you want to work. Use the Careers Information Room or general careers websites to get an idea of what the work involves and what skills and personal qualities employers look for. This will enable you to tailor the CV and bring out your own experience relevantly. If you are planning to send the same CV to a number of prospective employers, you should personalise the covering letter by putting in a paragraph on why you want to work for that organisation. The letter, though general, should appear to be specific to the position that the company is recruiting for. You may visit the following website that discusses points relating to the content and style of covering letters and CVs: www.kent.ac.uk/careers/cv/cvexamples.htm.

E-mailed CVs: Many employers accept applications in a CV format through e-mail. You should send them your CV as an attachment to an e-mail with a covering letter in the main body.

Format this e-mail in plain text so that it can be read by any e-mail reader. The CV is normally typed in MS Word (.doc) format, though Rich Text Format (.rtf) and web page format (.html) are acceptable alternatives. Do not forget to mention that you will send a printed CV (hard copy), if required. To make your CV look better, you may make convert it to a PDF (portable document format) file also. To check how this format is displayed, you may e-mail it back to yourself.

CV Templates

You may use Microsoft's templates to get an idea of the American style templates in use by downloading them from http://microsoft.com/en-us/templates. For British style templates, you may refer to www.businessballs.com or write your own CV with the help of the following format.

Heading

A CV should start with the heading 'Curriculum Vitae of ……………………' (your name without any title like Mr, Ms, etc.)

Personal Profile (and/or Attributes)

You may write a few high impact statements that describe the kind of person you are. These statements should reflect your personal strengths most suitable for the job that you have applied to. If you have a qualification relevant to the job, make that the final point. Some useful words and phrases are given below:

- I am a decisive and results-driven person who has… (mention the results that you have produced so far).
- Based on my experience of solving the problems relating to a family dispute regarding the distribution of property which I solved amicably for all the parties involved, I can say that I am a creative problem-solver as well as team-player.

Some other useful words and phrases are: technically competent/qualified (state discipline or area), commercially experienced and aware, task-orientated, excellent inter-personal and communications skills, sound planning and organisational capabilities, loyal and determined, etc.

Experience (and/or Specialisms or Capabilities)

In this section provide a description of your experience in bulleted points. Do not write a career history. You may also enumerate your capabilities. These simple statements (as shown in the examples given below) should be made to meet the requirements of your prospective employer. While making these points, you should sound confident and positive.

In case you are just beginning your career immediately after the completion of your education and have no or very little work experience, you should examine other aspects of your life's experience—your college or university experience, your hobbies, social or sports achievements, and bring out the relevant aspects of your experience that suit the job requirements like sharing responsibility, integrity, enthusiasm, initiative, creativity, etc. For example, think about cost-management that you might have done in organising the college annual day function or the people-skills that you may have developed in managing the debating society of your college. Put all these down in impressive statements. Use the active form of tense in writing these statements about yourself.

Achievements

In this section write compact, impressive statements highlighting your major achievements with facts and dates so that the prospective employer may verify them, if she/he wishes to do so. Vague claims without facts and figures and quantitative information will diminish your chances of employment. These achievements should back up the claims in the personal profile section discussed earlier.

Career History

Write a short paragraph on the history of your career starting with the most recent or present job and end with your first job. This may also be done through bullet points, each point highlighting a company, position, etc. Mention starting and finishing years, not necessarily the months, with company name, and city. Mention your job title(s). If you have very little work experience you can combine career history with other paragraphs.

Personal Details

Provide details like full name, sex, postal address, phone and mobile numbers, e-mail address, date of birth, marital status and education (school, college, university with the subjects that you have studied, class and dates). Mention two or three references, who know you either as a student or a colleague. Keep all this information very tight, compact and concise. If you are at a more advanced stage of your career you may not mention all the personal details mentioned above as some will be implicit or not relevant. Date the CV, and save as a file with some indication of what type of job it was orientated for, as you may develop a number of different CV's keeping in mind the requirements of your prospective employers.

Given below are two sample CVs, one for a senior position and the other for an entry-level, junior position.

Sample 1 (Senior Position)

Amit Gupta – Curriculum Vitae

Personal profile

- Experienced and innovative general manager with sophisticated sales, customer service and business administration skills
- High personal integrity, and able to relate to and create trust in all
- Highly articulate, confident and persuasive team-builder, able to motivate and communicate to achieve exceptional business performance
- Dependable and reliable in supporting and enabling team effort to produce genuine long-term sustainable development
- Persistent and flexible approach to the mutually beneficial achievement of business plans and personal goals of staff, suppliers and customers
- Honours degree in Mechanical Engineering

Experience

- Over 20 years proven expertise in industrial purchasing, manufacturing, logistics, business development, marketing, sales and service
- Background in a wide range of industries, including construction, plant hire, pharmaceutical, hygiene services and industrial process control
- Executive accountability for strategic planning, staffing, and sales development, etc., for a $60m international technology business
- International General Manager since 1991
- Management of change within the demanding and pressurised business environment
- Implementation of modern management practices, concerning personnel, IT, reporting systems, and partnership customer-supplier relations, etc.

Achievements

- As Production Control Executive with XYZ Corporation introduced PC-based systems to reduce lead-times from 7 months to 3 days, and inventory by 80% from $4.7m to $7.5m
- As Materials Manager with ABC Inc. introduced systems to reduce lead-times from 3 months to 7 days, and inventory from $6m to $2.5m, and achieved 12% reduction in $12m procurement costs
- As Operations Manager with Newco Inc. achieved 10% reduction in £7m procurement costs
- As General Manager for Bigco Int. business achieved growth from $800k to £5m, increased ne.. customer growth from 20 to 600 per annum

Career history

- 1973–88 Early career development with Newco Inc., Bigco Int., Mainco Plc.
- 1988–91 ABC Inc. as International Operations Manager
- 1991–present XYZ Corp. as General Manager

Personal details

Amit P. Gupta
H-128, Greater Kailash-I
New Delhi 110 048
Tel: 011- 2 971 5900
Email: amit@gmail.com

Date of Birth 09.09.53

Education

Delhi Public School 1965–72, St Stephen's College 1972–73, Delhi University School of Economics 1973–1977.

References are available on request.

December 2010

CV Sample 2 (Entry Level)

Nishi Sharma
D-54, Ratna Society
A-3 Surya Towers
Teen Rasta
Vadodara - 390 004
9824437218
nishi.sharma@yahoo.com

Objective

An entry-level marketing or management position with a medium-sized business.

Education

Bachelor of Science, Business Administration
M S University, Vadodara

- Major: Management
- Minor: Marketing

Related course work: personnel management, business management, business ethics, business law, macro economics, statistics, marketing and sales.

Expected: June 2010

Skills/Abilities

Management

- Developed and implemented new fund-raising program for social fraternity, which brought in more than Rs 30,000 for local charity
- Worked with local and national alumni chapters to coordinate renovation of college auditorium, including negotiating a construction contract and schedule
- Organised fund-raising program, which to date has brought in enough to cover 50% of expansion costs
- Managed Arts Club Treasury for two years
- Carried a full course load while serving as Arts Club Secretary and working on campus newspaper as proof reader

Sales

- Led campus newspaper advertising staff three consecutive years and generated all-time highest revenue
- Organised and implemented advertising promotion, which increased number of advertisers by 45%

Communication

- Presented monthly financial reports to Arts Club members and quarterly reports to college management committee
- Corresponded with chapter alumni on progress of auditorium expansion and renovation

References References are available on request
Dated 3 January 2010

WHAT MAKES A GOOD CV?

There is no one 'correct' way to write and present a CV but the following general rules may be followed:

- A CV is **targeted on the specific job** or career area for which you are applying and brings out the relevant skills you have to offer.
- It is carefully and **clearly laid out**: logically ordered, easy to read and not cramped.
- It is **informative, though concise.**
- It is **accurate in content, spelling and grammar.**
- It should be well typed on good quality paper.
- It should have a covering letter.

HOW LONG SHOULD A CV BE?

There are no absolute rules on this. However, in general, a new graduate's CV should cover **no more than two sides of A4 paper.** A more experienced applicant may write a fuller CV with a one page executive summary. If you can summarise your career history comfortably on a **single side**, this is desirable. However, you should not leave out important items, or crowd your text too closely together in order to fit it onto that single side. **Academic and technical CVs may be longer** as they have to show the experience and technical qualifications in detail.

CV COVER LETTERS

CV cover letters must be presented in an extremely professional manner. Use a good quality letter headed paper, and ensure that the name and address details and date appear correctly on the letter. **Do not use photocopies of a CV that you have already used. Do not use photocopied CV cover letters because they do not look personalised for the job concerned.**

Before you prepare the CV cover letter, look at what the job advertisement is seeking. Ensure that the required key skills, attributes and experience are reflected in the cover letter as well as your CV. Draw the reader's attention to the fact that your profile fits their requirements. Make the cover letter look like a special and direct response to the job advertisement and like a business letter. The quality of your cover letter presentation reflects how you write and present yourself. It is therefore advisable to include key words and phrases which reflect what the reader is seeking in a prospective employee.

Sample CV cover letters

As mentioned above the cover letters should be laid out neatly on good quality letterhead paper with your own address top-right or centre-top. You can create your own letterhead. However, avoid the use of fancy fonts and upper case (capital letters) where unnecessary. Use a single font in 10-12pt size. Given below is a sample cover letter, written in an assertive tone reflecting the nature of the applicant who is a goal-oriented achiever.

Sample 1

[Your Name]
[Street Address]
[Street Address 2]
[State, Pincode]
[Phone number]
[E-mail address]
March 1, 2009
[Recipient Name]
[Title]
[Company Name]
[Street Address]
[Street Address 2]
[City, State, Pincode]

Dear Mr / Ms **[Recipient Name]**,
I am a **[job title]** with **[number of years experience]** years of experience, and I am a perfect match for the position you advertised in **[location of advertisement]**.

Here is a description of how my experience compares with your requirements.

Job requirements	My experience
[Job requirement]	[Your experience]
[Job requirement]	[Your experience]
[Job requirement]	[Your experience]

As requested in your advertisement, I am including my salary requirements in this reply. They range from Rs **[lowest salary requirement]** to Rs **[highest salary requirement]** and are contingent upon a variety of factors such as the responsibilities of the position and the benefits offered.

I would welcome the opportunity to further discuss my skills and this position. If you have questions or would like to schedule an interview, please contact me on the phone at **[your phone number]** or by e-mail at **[your e-mail address]**. Please find enclosed my CV for your review. I look forward to hearing from you.

Sincerely,
[Your Name]

Enclosure

[Your Name]
[Street Address]
[City, State, PIN Code]

March 1, 2009

[Recipient Name]
[Title]
[Company Name]
[Street Address]
[City, State, PIN Code]

Sample 2

This is a cover letter for the position of a Secretary.

Your Name

Full Address (with name of the street, number of house/flat, name of city, and Pin Code)

Dear [**Recipient Name**]:

I am writing in response to your advertisement for a secretary in the *Indian Express* dated 10 July 2010. I shall be thankful if I could be granted an interview to enable me to demonstrate how my abilities fit your needs perfectly.

As you would see from the enclosed resume, I am proficient in a variety of computer software programs as well as in stenography. I have experience in handling general office duties. My excellent inter-personal and communication skills will help me discharge my duties effectively.

In me, you'll discover a reliable and extremely hard-working employee with a keen eye for detail.

You may contact me at [your phone number], to schedule an interview.

Sincerely,

[**Your Name**]

Enclosure

CV cover letters for unadvertised positions or opportunities

If you have come to know about a potential employer who may not have advertised for the position, you may send a speculative CV to that employer. As your application is not in response to any advertisement, address it to the senior person responsible for staffing decisions in the area you wish to apply to. Do not send the application without the name of a senior officer. In case you do not know the name of the concerned person, call up the company to find out the correct name and address details. In these cases obviously you are not likely to know precisely what skills they are seeking for, however, you may imagine the attributes that they might need and prepare your CV accordingly. Mention two or three of these attributes in your cover letter that best match your own profile and their likely interest. Look at the example given below.

[Your Name]

[Street Address]

[Street Address 2]

[City, State, PIN Code]

[Phone number]

[E-mail address]

March 1, 2010

[Recipient Name]

[Title]

[Company Name]

[Street Address]

[Street Address 2]

[City, State, PIN Code]

Dear [Recipient Name]:

If you are looking for a [job title] with:

- [number of years in the field] years of hands-on experience in [area of experience]
- knowledge of the latest technology in [industry or field]
- excellent written and oral communication skills
- a passion to learn and to increase skills

Kindly consider my application. You will see from my enclosed resume that I meet all of these qualifications and more.

I would very much like to discuss opportunities with **[Company Name]**. To schedule an interview, please call me at **[your phone number]**.

Thank you for taking the time to review my resume. I look forward to hearing from you.

Sincerely,

[Your Name]

Enclosure

You must have noticed that cover letters are short and concise. If you send a CV without a cover letter, people may not notice or read it. Writing a short, concise, hard-hitting cover letter also shows confidence and professionalism. You may write a long cover letter only if the job demands it. By being brief, you also have to be precise and describe your achievements in a few words that reflect your humility. Your CV and cover letter must be written in a simple language, in a no-nonsense manner so that they are easy to read.

TIPS ON CV PRESENTATION

- Your CV should be carefully and clearly laid out. It should neither be too cramped nor too short. Use bold and italic typefaces for headings and important information.
- Do not type on the back of a page. Each page should be on a separate sheet of paper. You may put your name in the footer area so that it appears on each sheet.
- Be concise. A CV is an appetiser and not a complete meal. It should reveal only as much as is needed for the reader to call you for an interview. Therefore, do not list every examination and every activity. Mention only the most relevant and/or impressive examinations, activities and experiences.
- Be positive. Put yourself across very confidently in your CV and highlight your strong points. For example, when listing your qualifications, put your highest academic qualifications and grades first.
- Be honest. Although a CV does allow you to omit details which you would prefer the employer not to know about, you should never give inaccurate or misleading information.
- If you are sending your CV through post/courier, do not fold it. Put it in a full-size A4 envelope so that it does not arrive creased.
- While typing your CV, use Times New Roman font as they are the most acceptable.

- Font size normally used is 12 points for the body text with larger sizes for subheadings and headings.

SUMMARY

To summarise, CV's are written to market yourself so that people know your worth and can utilise your services to grow and help you grow along with them. But this does not mean that once you have sent your CV you have secured a job. The main purpose behind writing a CV is to help organisations understand your potential and capabilities so that there is no hesitation in calling you for an interview or a one-to-one talk/discussion. It is extremely important therefore to write an effective CV and to create a mark for your self and set a context before the final personal interview.

Activities

1. Draft a letter of application and a detailed a CV for the following advertisements:

WANTED

- Leading Bank having 51 branches in Raigad District requires senior officers in Accounts & Audit Section
- Age group between 40–45, minimum 10 years experience in banking
- Graduates/Postgraduates need apply. Salary as per the qualification and experience
- Please send applications with all relevant documents to:

M. S. Modak,Chartered Accountant,
6/B Jamshetji Road, Near Shiv Sena Bhavan
Mahim, Mumbai 400 016

Glenmark Generics Limited

Glenmark Generics Limited is a research-led, global, fully integrated pharmaceutical company headquarted in Mumbai.

The company has generic formulation and API business interests in more than 80 countries across the world. We have the following vacancies at our Kurkumbh and Mohol API Facility.

Jr Officer/Officer (Production): BE/BTech (Chemical) or BSc/MSc (Chemical) with 2–9 years of experience in bulk drugs manufacturing.

Officer (Engineering): BE/BTech (Electrical) with 3–7 years of relevant experience.

Interested candidates may email their CV to aramb@glenmark-generics.com or post it to Glenmark Generics Ltd A-80, MIDC, Kurkumbh, Daund, Pune.

2. What is a CV and what is its main function?
3. What points should you bear in mind while writing the cover letter?
4. 'An application letter is a sales letter'. State your views on this statement.

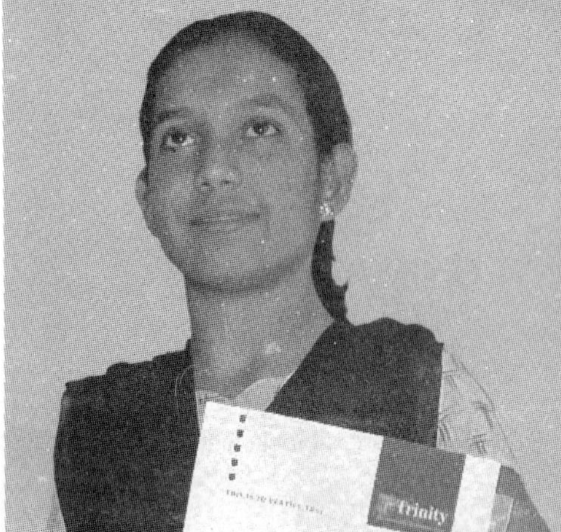